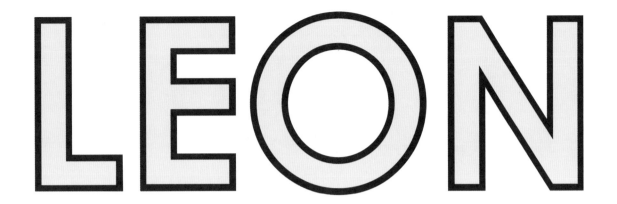

LEON

HAPPY GUTS

Recipes to help you live better

BY REBECCA SEAL & JOHN VINCENT

conran OCTOPUS

CONTENTS

INTRODUCTION

LEON is all about happy tummies. When we opened our first restaurant, back in 2004, our mission was to provide everyone with naturally fast food – food that majored on rainbow-coloured, fibre-filled plants. While we might not have known quite as much about gut health then as we do now, our food has always been the kind of food that can contribute to a happy gut. A happy gut can mean a longer, healthier, life. And who doesn't want that?

Over the years, we've learned a lot about the gut and what it needs, which is why we decided to put this book together. The recipes are, as ever, from all over the world, and we had a lot of fun looking for the best high-fibre dishes, for the most colourful recipes and for the simplest ways to eat gut-supporting omega-3 fatty acids. We won't insist you give anything up or change your diet completely. Instead, we hope that inside this book you will find things so tasty and so irresistible that eating in a gut-healthy way turns out to be both easy and unmissably delicious.

Rebecca and John x

EAT THE RAINBOW

EAT FOODS CONTAINING LIVE MICROBES

EAT MORE FIBRE

OMEGA-3

EAT LESS SUGAR & SALT

EAT LESS MEAT

EAT SLOWLY & CONSCIOUSLY

INTERMITTENT FASTING

EXERCISE, RELAX & SLEEP

HOW TO KEEP YOUR GUT HAPPY

We are as individual on the inside as we are on the outside. The science of gut health is new and evolving, but what we do know for sure is that we all need a happy, healthy and diverse community of good gut bacteria. They work with both our immune system and the gut itself, help our brains to function and look after our long-term health, as well as how we feel day-to-day. (Of course, some branches of traditional medicine, like Ayurveda, have been saying similar things for rather longer. In some ways, the science is simply catching up with what many have practised for centuries.)

Sadly, the modern 'Western' diet in general, with its focus on refined carbs, processed meat and lots of (often hidden) sugars, means that our good gut bacteria are nowhere near as diverse or numerous as they need to be. As diets worldwide become more Westernized, gut diversity is decreasing everywhere, and health outcomes are getting worse.

Fortunately, there are some very simple ways we can all make our gut microbiome happier – which is why we've written this book.

You can just follow our recipes, and the guidelines on the next page – making whatever swaps and switches you need – but if you want to know a bit more about the science of gut health and exactly what ingredients to eat more of and why, read the next few pages, too.

We want to make eating for a happy gut delicious, easy and, most importantly, joyful – because a joyful diet means a happy body.

THE KEYS TO GUT HEALTH

EAT THE RAINBOW Good gut bacteria not only feed off the polyphenols (a category of plant compounds with significant health benefits) that we deliver them by eating colourful food, but also turn them into nutrients we need, and can't get anywhere else. We don't just mean nuts, berries and greens – polyphenols also exist in dark chocolate, red wine, good-quality olive oil, coffee and tea.

EAT MORE FIBRE Good gut bacteria thrive on fibre, so we need to eat a range of whole grains, legumes and vegetables to keep them happy. Many fibre-rich foods are considered 'prebiotic' and create the right environment for 'probiotic' good bacteria. Eating more fibre also means there will be less space in your diet for highly refined carbs – think swapping white rice for red or black rice, or breakfast cereals for multigrain-and-seed granola.

EAT FOODS CONTAINING LIVE MICROBES These foods will contain the very bacteria we want to help thrive in our guts. While you can take these bacteria as tablets or powders, they are also found in particularly tasty foods, especially fermented goodies which generally contain a wide variety of different types of bacteria. Try unpasteurized cheeses, live yoghurts, kimchi, pickles, miso, kefir, kombucha and sauerkraut.

OMEGA-3 The connection between omega-3 fatty acids and gut health is a new one, but studies show omega-3 increases diversity in the gut and also enables gut bacteria to release very beneficial natural anti-inflammatory compounds. Omega-3 is found in oily fish, flaxseeds/linseeds and their oil, some nuts and tofu.

EAT LESS SUGAR & SALT A sugar-rich diet can displace other nutritious foods, and of course, keeping sugar levels low and steady is good for the rest of the body, too. It has been suggested that a high-salt diet may impact the health of the gut microbiome after a recent study found that reducing salt in the diet possibly helped to improve heart health by reducing blood pressure through the gut.

EAT SLOWLY & CONSCIOUSLY Eating is a complex set of actions for the body, which it needs enough time to do. Eating quickly and thoughtlessly means we miss the signals telling us when we are full.

EAT LESS MEAT By eating less meat and choosing pastured, grass-fed meat when we do, we naturally make more room for plants (and maybe fish) on our plates.

DON'T EAT AT ALL A recipe book might be a strange place to talk about fasting, but the science is clear: occasional fasts, even as short as 16 hours, give our gut bacteria time to recover and grow. John and Rebecca both fast regularly – for Rebecca, this just means an early evening meal followed by a late breakfast, two or three times a week.

EXERCISE, RELAX & SLEEP Studies show that exercise can help keep our gut microbes happy, as can taking time to de-stress, and getting enough sleep. Tired, stressed-out people often have tired, stressed-out guts, as well.

WHAT IS IT ABOUT THE MODERN WESTERN DIET?

When we talk about the 'Western' diet, it is no longer a geographic description. Instead, it describes a diet that has spread worldwide, one that relies heavily on highly processed foods full of very refined white carbs (meaning the fibre has been removed), lots of additives and not much in the way of naturally occurring micronutrients. It's a diet high in processed versions of meat and dairy and very high in sugars, often hidden in unexpected products, like readymeals, bread products, hot drinks and packet sauces. It's also low in oily fish, healthy fats, whole grains, nuts, seeds, fresh fruit, vegetables and fibre.

As diets go, it couldn't really be worse for gut health, since it doesn't usually contain a wide enough range of the nutrients a diverse gut microbiome needs to survive, and is full of the sugars that allow some microbes to grow and overwhelm other important but less sturdy ones. There's even some evidence to suggest that added ingredients such as emulsifiers and artificial sweeteners can upset our microbial balance.

In contrast, traditional diets that depend heavily on whole foods, relatively unrefined carbohydrates and plants, and that contain a certain amount of fish and meat, tend to result in diverse gut bacteria. The so-called Mediterranean diet is, of course, a Western diet (and Mediterranean countries are not immune to the pull of the hyper-modern, highly processed diet) but those who eat a true Mediterranean diet still tend to eat lots of fresh produce, whole grains, legumes, oily fish and olive oil – hence its reputation from several huge meta studies for resulting in good health and a long life, as well as from more recent research into better mental health. The same may be true, though, for many other plant-rich traditional diets, whether from India, Scandinavia, Japan or southern America – which is why we collect recipes from all over the world.

WHAT DO OUR MICROBES DO?

A good way to understand gut microbes is to think about cows. Have you ever wondered how a cow can possibly make milk, and potentially be turned into such rich and flavourful meat, when it only eats leaves? The answer is microbes. Like all mammals, cows have a symbiotic relationship with their gut microbes, which evolved over millions of years alongside cows, to the extent that they can liberate nutrients from grass that the cow's gut alone cannot.

The same is true for humans: our trillions of symbiotic microbes do jobs that our guts are not equipped to do. Some of them synthesize essential vitamins, like B vitamins and vitamin K, and amino acids for us; others ferment or co-metabolize foods to help our bodies get at their nutrients; still others fight off pathogens. They are also involved in maintaining our immune system and they impact on other organs of the body, as well as protecting the structures of the gut itself. Having too many or too few of certain microbes even seems to predispose us to obesity, and the kinds of behaviours that give rise to it. Given all this, it makes sense that if the thousand or so species of microbes that live in our guts become unbalanced, by poor diet, stress, lack of exercise or sleep, or by over-use of medications such as antibiotics, all sorts of things can go wrong.

To find out more about our microbes, we recommend Tim Spector's books, *The Diet Myth* and *Spoon Fed – Why Almost Everything We've been Told About Food Is Wrong*. Also, *10% Human* by Allana Collen – the title refers to the number of microbes living in or on our bodies, compared to the number of cells we are made up of.

THE GUT-BRAIN AXIS

There is no doubt that our guts and brains are tightly connected, nor that mood and food are closely linked – think about the butterflies we feel when we're nervous or excited, or the churning in our stomachs when stressed. The gut has its own nervous system, the enteric nervous system, which has more neurones and nerves than many small animal brains do. However, detailed examination of the implications of all this has only been going on for a couple of decades. What we know is that the vagus nerve connects the brain and the gut (it also connects to other organs), mostly sending necessary messages to and from the gut to the brain about things like fullness or digestion.

We also know that the vagus nerve, like all nerves, carries neurotransmitter chemicals – little blurts of serotonin, dopamine, adrenaline or oxytocin – from the gut to the brain. The intriguing thing is that we now know microbes can generate their own feel-good neurotransmitters too, which also whizz up the vagus nerve to the brain. Work is on-going to discover more, but it's another way in which microbes play a critical role in our well-being. It's early days, but initial research has looked at things such as sleep improving due to probiotic consumption, as well as examining the role of dysbiosis (a microbial imbalance in the gut) in apparently unrelated conditions, such as autism, Parkinson's disease and depression. It even appears that over-growth of less helpful bacteria can affect our behaviour – having too much of the wrong kind of microbes has even been suggested to impact upon our food cravings, for example.

WHAT THIS BOOK IS NOT

This is not a diet book. It is not a weight-loss book. We like you just the way you are. Instead, it's about eating in a way that might just keep us all healthy and happy for longer.

It is also not a FODMAP (Fermentable Oligo-, Di-, Mono-saccharides And Polyols) book. For some people who have IBS or other gut disorders, following a low-FODMAP diet leads to a reduction in their symptoms. It's a complicated and quite restrictive diet, that should only be attempted with support from a specialist dietitian, as it involves avoiding a lot of the ingredients that those without gut disorders usually need to eat more of: legumes, fruits and grains, among other things. If you follow your own version of a FODMAP diet, you will already know how to adapt our recipes. However, where onions and garlic are optional – since avoiding alliums is something many FODMAPers find an easy win – we have noted it. For the rest of us, garlic and onions tend to be good for gut health.

KEY INGREDIENTS

GENERAL whole grains (oats, quinoa, freekeh, bulghur wheat berries) • tofu • legumes • lentils • nuts (including ground and nut butters) • seeds, including sesame and flaxseeds/linseeds • extra virgin olive oil, sesame oil, coconut oil, flax oil • uncooked and unpasteurized cheeses • brown, red and black rice • raw vinegars • kimchi, sauerkraut, fermented pickles • oily fish (including traditionally smoked), tinned fish, shellfish and seafood • dark chocolate • live crème fraîche, live full-fat yoghurt (or live non-dairy alternative), labneh • cocoa • gram flour, buckwheat, rye flour • couscous (cold) • potatoes (cold) • tahini • kefir

VEGETABLES beetroot • beans • asparagus • fennel • garlic • carrots • leeks • white and red cabbage • leaves (especially bitter) • herbs • sweet potatoes • artichokes • olives • chicory • black beans • spinach • red onions • white beans • mushrooms • tomatoes • Brussels sprouts • seaweed • kale • broccoli • celeriac • peppers • courgette • squash • cauliflower • Asian greens • radishes • mooli/daikon

FRUITS stone fruits • berries • pomegranates • melons • dried fruit • apples • pears • bananas • citrus

FLAVOURINGS capers • ginger • cinnamon • cloves • anise • chilli • turmeric • cumin • paprika • miso paste • tamari/fermented soy sauce • live fermented hot sauces • fermented pickles

INGREDIENT TIPS

• Use extra virgin olive oil with abandon (for its polyphenols), along with rapeseed oil, which is great for cooking, as well as walnut oil, flax oil and avocado oil in dressings. These give us a range of good, healthy fats, which – along with our brains and bodies – our gut microbes also need.

• Use unpasteurized cheeses and live yoghurts (look for the word 'bio' on the label), including those made without dairy, with no added sugar or sweeteners. While chilling them doesn't affect their probiotic nature (you can even freeze them), cooking them kills the good bacteria. Fermented milks, kefir and kombucha are also great sources of gut-friendly bacteria.

• Keep the skin on your fruit and veg wherever possible, as it's where most of the gut-friendly fibre is. Give them a quick scrub under running water to remove any dirt.

• Serve potatoes, rice, pasta, bulgur, freekeh and couscous in cold dishes, rather than hot – cooling the starch changes it, turning it into resistant starch, which our microbes love. You don't have to give up refined carbs for a gut-healthy lifestyle.

• Choose sourdough-based wholegrain breads where you can. While cooking sourdough kills the live microbes that are beneficial for gut health, they've already done much of their gut-friendly work during rising and proving, releasing nutrients that our stomachs alone would struggle to access and, for some people, making the bread as a whole easier to digest, too.

• Take joy in the fact that red wine, coffee, green tea and dark chocolate all contain phytochemicals (a.k.a. antioxidants), a wide range of micronutrients that our gut microbes thrive on, breaking them down into useful metabolites, which our bodies then use.

SOME GOOD NEWS ABOUT WINE & CHEESE (& SOME BEERS)

For years, the Mediterranean diet confounded experts – because, along with all the good stuff, its adherents also seem to get away with eating an awful lot of cheese (the average French person eats 500g per week), washed down with lots of red wine. More recently, data suggests that these two things may actually be part of what makes the Mediterranean lifestyle so successful.

First, unpasteurized cheese – the kind mostly eaten in Mediterranean countries – tends to be absolutely teeming with beneficial live bacteria. We used to think that these were destroyed by stomach acid, but it now seems that they may in fact survive well into the gut. It's not hard to get unpasteurized cheeses, as many given a label of Protected Designation of Origin, such as Brie, Camembert, Parmigiano Reggiano or Roquefort, have to be made in the old-fashioned, unpasteurized way. Where possible, don't cook them, though (see page 134 for more on that).

Secondly, red wine is a fantastic source of polyphenols (see page 15 for more on why polyphenols are great). And certain bottle-conditioned beers have also been shown to be as lively as yoghurt.

Obviously, you should both drink and consume cheese in moderation. You can have too much of a very good thing.

HOW TO GET MORE FIBRE INTO YOUR DIET

In the 1980s, when Rebecca was little, high-fibre diets were all the rage, and her mum used to sprinkle a spoonful of bran fibre onto her morning Readybrek, which tasted like sawdust. Today, our understanding of fibre is a little better (although, like all nutritional science, there's plenty more to unravel).

Ideally, we need to eat about 30g of fibre a day. Many fibre-rich foods (as well as some foods not rich in fibre, such as dark chocolate and coffee) are also rich in useful antioxidant polyphenols, especially those which are dark or red in colour, such as dark leafy greens or beetroot. In this book, we have deliberately used lots of high-fibre ingredients — from oats and chickpeas, to almonds and artichokes. An easy way to eat more fibre is to slowly decrease your intake of low-fibre foods — things made from refined white wheat flour, skinless white potatoes, white rice and fruit juices — and gradually fill the gaps with higher-fibre alternatives.

2 slices of sourdough
bread = 5g

50g oats = 5g

1 tablespoon
almond butter
= 1.6g

50g carrot sticks = 1.4g

WHAT DOES 30G OF FIBRE LOOK LIKE?

50g cooked Puy lentils = 7.5g

100g blueberries = 2.5g

80g peas = 4g

50g hummus = 3g

HOW TO GET STARTED

Humans are great at thinking big, but when it comes to acting on our ideas, we quickly get overwhelmed and revert to our usual ways. With gut health, start with one or two small steps first – this is good for your willpower, as well as your body.

It could be changing your breakfast to Bircher Muesli (see page 23) or granola, with lots of fresh or dried fruit, making life easy by

batch-making what you need for a week of breakfasts on a Sunday evening. It could be giving up ham sandwiches and making a range of rainbow sandwiches and salads for lunch (see pages 86 and 98). It could be swapping your regular boiled potatoes for a different vegetable side dish every night. Or, it could be as simple as having a bottle of homemade Water Kefir (page 154) in the fridge, or giving up on sliced white and choosing wholemeal sourdough bread (see page 128), instead.

TAKE IT SLOW
One thing that is becoming more

and more clear, as nutritional science develops, is that people do best with a personalized diet. What works for you may not work for someone else. Some of us do well on lactose; others feel sluggish after eating wheat. There is no one-size-fits-all diet, and you should pay close attention to how the food you eat really makes you feel, getting to know your body and its needs. (We don't recommend cutting out whole food groups without professional support.)

However, if there's one piece of advice that truly does fit everyone, it's this: don't rush into a new gut-healthy lifestyle too quickly. Give your gut time to adapt. Rapidly increasing the amount of fibre you eat – especially if you don't eat much to start with – means your gut won't be prepared and will potentially lead to un-fun symptoms that will stop you wanting to carry on. The same goes for live microbe-rich foods such as kefir and kombucha – even if it's love at first taste, start with small servings over several days, allowing your gut to adjust to its change in occupants.

POLYPHENOLS & WHY EATING COLOURFULLY IS GOOD FOR US

Polyphenols are found in all sorts of plant foods, and eating a wide range of them has been shown to be good for general health. Some have strong antioxidant and anti-inflammatory effects, such as flavanoids, which – hurrah! – are found in highest concentrations in cocoa. (This is why we've created a comparatively low-sugar, cocoa-rich cake, see page 188.) In fact, part of the long-running UK Twins Study recently found that people who had high blood-flavanoid levels, coming from chocolate, berries and wine, also had lower blood pressure, stronger bones and a lower risk of diabetes[1].

We have known for a while that diets rich in things such as blueberries and broccoli seem to be especially good for us, but it's only recently that scientists have discovered how our gut microbes use various polyphenols to create other valuable chemicals, which our bodies then absorb and use – things like butyrate (a type of short-chain fatty acid), which nourishes the vital cells lining the walls of our gut (lower levels of butyrate may even be associated with certain bowel diseases).

WHY SO MANY NUTS?

You will notice that this book contains a lot of nuts. This is because nuts are a great source of a range of polyphenols – in fact, Americans get up to two-thirds of their entire polyphenol intake from peanuts – and some nuts, such as walnuts, are excellent sources of omega-3, as well. All nuts contain valuable bundles of other nutrients, such as vitamin E (almonds), selenium (Brazil nuts) and magnesium (cashews), as well zinc, calcium and B vitamins.

[1]*The Diet Myth*, Tim Spector, W&N, 2015, page 208.

RECIPE KEY

WF
WHEAT FREE

GF
GLUTEN FREE

DF
DAIRY FREE

Ve
VEGAN

V
VEGETARIAN

NF
NUT FREE

SoF
SOY FREE

SUITABLE FOR FREEZING

WAYS TO EAT MORE FIBRE

Our good gut bacteria love fibre, and
they liberate nutrients from it for us, too
(but very few of us eat enough).

BUCKWHEAT PANCAKES

SERVES 4 (makes about 12)

PREP TIME: 4 MINS * COOK TIME: 20–30 MINS, depending on how many pancakes you can cook at a time

V | NF | SoF

75g **buckwheat flour**
75g **plain flour**
1½ teaspoons **baking powder**
1 tablespoon **sugar**
a pinch of **salt**
125ml **milk** (any kind)
1 **egg**
1 tablespoon flavourless **oil**, plus
    extra for cooking
½ teaspoon **vanilla bean paste**
zest of ¼ **lemon**

TO SERVE:
fresh berries or defrosted **frozen fruit**
thick plain live **yoghurt** (any kind)
a drizzle of **maple syrup**

≡TIP≡

Experiment with
other fruits:
homemade apple
purée, sliced banana,
fresh peaches…

Buckwheat has nothing to do with wheat, despite its name – it is known as a pseudocereal, since it's like one, but isn't. Its seeds have been used in cooking for thousands of years. We use it to make light, fluffy, slightly nutty breakfast pancakes, which can easily be made gluten-free with a quick swap of the plain flour and baking powder for GF alternatives.

Mix the dry ingredients together in a large bowl. In a separate bowl, beat together the milk, egg, 1 tablespoon of oil, vanilla bean paste and lemon zest. Pour the wet mixture into the dry bowl and stir to combine, making sure no lumps remain. Because this has no gluten, there's no need to let the batter rest – it's best to cook it immediately while the baking powder is most active.

Place a large frying pan over a medium heat. Add as little oil as possible, just enough to barely coat the base. When the pan and oil are hot, use a large spoon to portion out the batter into the pan, making thick pancakes around 8cm across. Cook until small bubbles appear on top and the bottom is golden brown, then flip and cook the other side. Set aside somewhere warm, like a low oven, or wrap in a clean tea towel while you cook the rest.

Eat immediately, while hot, with fruit, yoghurt and a little maple syrup.

UTTERLY NUTTERLY

You can use most nuts to make nut butter. As you're in control of what goes in, you'll avoid the extra salt, sugar and even palm oil that many brands contain. We prefer to use blanched nuts as you get a smoother butter, but you can use skin-on for the fibre, if you like.

If you have a high-powered blender, it should make quick work of most nuts, but sometimes you may have to add a little extra fat to bring it together – and big blenders won't cope well with small quantities either. A small hand-held food processor can work just as well as a jug blender. If you do need to loosen a dry butter, add the fat very slowly and stick to something that is solid at room temperature. Although we almost always advocate olive oils for gut health, coconut oil is good here because it's solid at room temperature and won't separate – we use about 1–3 teaspoons of refined flavourless coconut oil.

CASHEW NUT BUTTER

MAKES 240G

PREP TIME: 15 MINS * COOK TIME: 12 MINS

WF | GF | DF | V | Ve | SoF

200g **raw (unroasted) cashews**
1–3 teaspoons **refined coconut oil** (optional)

TO FLAVOUR:
a pinch of **sea salt**, **sugar**, **maple syrup** or **agave**, to taste

Heat the oven to 175°C/350°F/gas mark 4.

Tip the nuts onto a baking sheet and roast in the oven for 8–12 minutes until pale golden, giving them a shimmy halfway through. Remove and allow to cool for a few minutes, then tip into a blender or small food processor. Process until the nuts have gone from pale and powdery to a thick, creamy spreadable butter – this can take 5–10 minutes. If the mixture refuses to butter up, add a tiny bit of oil to get it going, but avoid this if possible.

Taste. You can leave the nut butter plain, or add a pinch of sea salt, or a little natural sweetness – just do it slowly, tasting as you go.

Store in a spotlessly clean jar or lidded tub, in a cool, dark place.

ALMOND BUTTER

MAKES 240G

PREP TIME: 15 MINS * COOK TIME: 15 MINS

WF | GF | DF | V | Ve | SoF

200g **blanched almonds**
1–3 teaspoons **refined coconut
    oil** (optional)

Follow the same method as opposite, but roast the nuts
for slightly longer, 12–15 minutes usually. Process in the
same way.

=TIP=

You can experiment with
all sorts of flavours and
combinations. Try hazelnut
butter with added vanilla
extract and melted dark
chocolate.

═TIP═

Apple juice is traditional but there are hundreds of ways to make overnight oats — you could soak them in any milk or yoghurt (coconut is good), add nut butter, roasted spelt flakes or barley flakes, vanilla extract or paste, chopped fruit, or finish with a little maple, honey or agave.

BIRCHER MUESLI

SERVES 2–3

PREP TIME: 8 MINS PLUS OVERNIGHT SOAKING

V | SoF

50g **porridge oats** (GF if necessary)

1 **eating/dessert apple**, coarsely grated

150ml **apple juice** (choose one made with whole fruit and no added sugar)

2 tablespoons **dried fruit** (**dates**, **raisins**, **sultanas**, **blueberries**, **cherries**, **apricots**), chopped if large

4 tablespoons chopped **mixed nuts** (**hazelnuts**, **almonds**, **walnuts**, **pecans**, **brazils**), ideally pre-roasted

a generous pinch of **ground flaxseeds/ linseeds** (not whole, they stick in your teeth)

milk (any kind), as needed

4 tablespoons **plain yoghurt** (any kind)

about 75g fresh or defrosted frozen **mixed berries** (**strawberries**, **raspberries**, **blueberries**, **blackberries**, **pomegranate seeds**), chopped if large, or a dollop of **fruit compote**

1 teaspoon each of **sunflower** and **pumpkin seeds**, to sprinkle

Bircher muesli is made by soaking oats and grated apple overnight in the fridge, meaning your breakfast will be almost ready the moment you wake up. Oats are a great source of fibre. including resistant starch, and soaking them seems to make them more digestible, which our microbes love.

If the texture is too soft for you – it is, naturally, porridgy – for extra crunch, batch-roast the nuts on a Sunday (200g at 175°C/350°F/gas mark 4 for 6–8 minutes) and toast 5 teaspoons of pumpkin seeds in a hot dry pan until they start to pop. Store in a sealed container and add just before serving – they will see you through until Friday.

The night before, mix the oats, grated apple and apple juice in a bowl. Place the bowl in the fridge overnight.

The next morning, stir in the dried fruit, chopped nuts and ground flaxseeds/ linseeds. If the mixture looks too thick, add a splash of milk to loosen it. Divide the mixture between 2 or 3 serving bowls and top each one with half of the yoghurt, fruit and seeds. Eat immediately.

CLASSIC WHOLEMEAL LOAF

MAKES 1 LOAF
PREP TIME: 20 MINS PLUS 2 HOURS RISING AND PROVING * COOK TIME: 40 MINS
DF | V | Ve | NF | SoF

500g **strong wholemeal flour**, plus extra
   for dusting
1 teaspoon **easy-bake yeast** (the kind that
   doesn't need activating first)
1 tablespoon **light brown sugar**
1½ teaspoons **salt**
340ml **lukewarm water**
2 tablespoons **extra virgin olive oil**, plus
   extra for greasing

You won't believe the difference in taste when you bake your own bread, nor how easy it is. Once you've mastered this simple recipe, experiment: we sometimes use spelt bread flour, or a mixture of wholemeal and strong white bread flour, or shape the bread into rolls on a baking sheet before the final prove (they only need 15–20 minutes cooking time, depending on their size).

In a large bowl, mix together the flour, yeast, sugar and salt. Add the water and oil and mix with your hands until lumpy and craggy. Tip out onto a lightly floured work surface and knead for 10 minutes until thoroughly combined (or use the dough hook attachment on your mixer). If you find it's too sticky, add a spoonful or so of flour. Lightly grease the mixing bowl, place the ball of dough back in, cover with a clean, damp tea towel and leave to rise in a warm place until doubled in size, about 1 hour.

Lightly knead the dough again for a couple of minutes before moulding into an oval and placing in a greased 900g/2 lb loaf tin. (If you don't have a tin, you can make a more rustic, round cottage loaf on a baking sheet.) Cover with the tea towel and leave to rise in a warm place until doubled in size, about 45 minutes.

Heat the oven to 200°C/400°F/gas mark 6.

Bake for 35–40 minutes, until you can easily take the loaf out of the tin. If you tap the base of the loaf and it sounds hollow, it is done.

Transfer to a wire rack to cool.

SPICY CHICKPEAS ON TOAST

SERVES 2
PREP TIME: 4 MINS * COOK TIME: 6 MINS
V | NF | SoF

2 tablespoons **olive oil**

1 heaped tablespoon **tomato purée**

1–2 cloves of **garlic**, crushed, to taste (optional)

400g **canned chickpeas**, in water, drained

1–2 teaspoons finely chopped **red chilli**, or to taste

1 teaspoon **sweet smoked paprika**

2 tablespoons **water**

freshly squeezed **lemon juice**, to taste

salt and **freshly ground black pepper**, to taste

TO SERVE:

2–4 slices of **wholegrain sourdough**, depending on their size

butter or good-quality **extra virgin olive oil**, for spreading or brushing

100g **ricotta** or **kefir cheese** (see introduction, page 155, or ready-made from a tub)

This is a step up from beans on toast in terms of flavour and nutrition (even though we do love beans on toast from time to time), but takes only a few minutes longer to make.

Set a saucepan over a medium heat. When hot, add the oil and then the tomato purée and garlic, if using (add lots if you love garlic, less or none if you don't). Cook, stirring, for 1–2 minutes until the garlic stops smelling pungent and raw, and the oil and purée blend together. Add the chickpeas, chilli and smoked paprika. Stir well and add the water, then cook for a further 2 minutes until everything is piping hot. Remove from the heat.

Toast the bread and butter it or brush with extra virgin olive oil.

Squeeze a little lemon juice into the chickpeas, mix and then taste. Add salt and pepper or more lemon juice, as needed. Pile the chickpeas onto the hot toast and crumble over the cheese. Eat immediately.

＝TIP＝

Obviously, vegans can leave out the cheese or use vegan cheeses. Any curd cheese or crumbly white cheese, or even cream cheese spread directly onto the toast, would be delicious with these spicy, smoky chickpeas.

LABLABI

SERVES 2

PREP TIME: 6 MINS * COOK TIME: 10 MINS

DF | NF | SoF

400g **canned chickpeas** in water

100ml **water**

1 clove of **garlic**, crushed

1 heaped teaspoon **harissa paste**, plus extra to serve

a pinch of **salt**

2 **eggs**

1 large slice of day-old **wholegrain sourdough bread** (or any stale **bread**), torn into rough pieces

about 75g **canned tuna** (ideally a good-quality one in olive oil)

1 teaspoon **ground cumin**, or more, to taste

2 heaped teaspoons **capers in brine**

extra virgin olive oil, for drizzling

freshly squeezed **lemon juice**, to taste

═TIP═

If you have time, soaking and cooking dried chickpeas from scratch and using their cooking liquor for the broth adds both texture and flavour – use about 125g dried chickpeas for 2 people.

This Tunisian dish is often called a soup, but it's too fantastically chunky for that to be the right word. Lablabi is, in fact, mostly eaten for breakfast or in cafés where the chickpeas are cooked to perfect tenderness overnight (consequently, our version is a bit short-cut heavy to be called authentic). Perhaps the best thing about lablabi – apart from its speedy prep and rich, spicy flavour – is that after you've arranged it prettily in a bowl, you have to smash it all together with your spoon before eating. Customize to your tastes: leave out the bread, or the egg, or the tuna. Some Tunisians add olives, others eat it with pickled vegetables, like carrot, stirred through, or on the side.

Pour the chickpeas and their water into a saucepan. Add the measured water, garlic, harissa paste and salt, stir and bring to a simmer.

Bring a separate pan of water to a simmer over a medium heat. Crack in the eggs and poach until just cooked, 2–4 minutes, depending on the eggs.

Divide the torn bread between 2 large soup bowls. Spoon the chickpeas and their broth over the bread and top with the poached eggs as soon as they are ready. Arrange the tuna next to the eggs and do the same with the cumin and capers. Add a generous spoonful of harissa paste to each bowl, to taste, then drizzle over a little extra virgin olive oil and a squeeze of lemon.

Once everything is in the bowls, bring to the table. Just before eating, break up the egg with a spoon and mix everything in the bowl together. After your first taste, you can add more harissa, lemon, cumin, salt or olive oil.

IRANIAN-STYLE EGGS WITH GARLICKY BEANS & DILL

SERVES 2

PREP TIME: 10 MINS PLUS OPTIONAL SOAKING TIME * COOK TIME: 35–40 MINS

WF | GF | DF | V | NF | SoF

80g **long-grain brown rice**, pre-soaked in cold water (see method)

2 tablespoons **olive oil**

2 cloves of **garlic**, crushed

400g **canned cannellini beans** in water, drained but not rinsed (or 240g **cooked cannellini beans**)

½ teaspoon **ground turmeric**

a big handful of roughly chopped **dill**

a big handful of roughly chopped **flat-leaf parsley**

a big handful of roughly chopped **coriander**

50g **spinach**, washed, stems removed and roughly chopped

2–4 **eggs**, depending on hunger

freshly squeezed lemon juice, to taste

salt and **freshly ground black pepper**

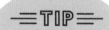

TIP

Vegans can double the beans and leave out the eggs, or scramble in some silken tofu in their place.

A combination of two Iranian egg-and-herb dishes, baghali ghatogh and torshi tareh, this is quick to cook and soothing to eat.

If you have time, soak the rice in cold water before cooking – any length of time will help, but if you put it in the fridge to soak in the morning, by dinnertime the rice will cook in just 20 minutes.

Drain the rice, place in a pan and cover with twice its volume of fresh cold water (or three times its volume if you didn't soak it). Bring to a simmer and cover with a lid. Cook for 20–35 minutes, or until tender. If there is water left in the pan, drain it, then fluff up the rice with a fork and cover with the lid again.

Meanwhile, heat the olive oil in a large grill-safe pan over a medium heat. Add the garlic and cook for 1 minute, stirring, then tip in the beans and turmeric. Cook for 1 minute, stirring, then add the herbs and spinach. Cook until the spinach is completely wilted.

When the rice is ready, preheat the grill to its highest setting. Make 2–4 wells in the spinach mixture, crack each egg into a small bowl or mug, then tip each one into a well. Let the bottoms of the eggs cook for 2–3 minutes, then – while the tops of the eggs are still very wobbly – slide the pan under the hot grill. Cook for just 1 minute or so until the tops of the eggs are set.

Divide the rice between serving bowls and serve the eggs, spinach and beans on top. Squeeze over a little lemon juice and finish with a little salt and pepper. Eat immediately.

EGG, CHICORY, FENNEL & POTATO SALAD

SERVES 2 AS A MAIN OR 4 WITH OTHER DISHES
PREP TIME: 10 MINS * COOK TIME: 12 MINS
WF | GF | NF | SoF

275g **new potatoes**, halved or quartered
    into equal-sized pieces
2 **eggs**
½ small head of **fennel**, finely sliced,
    fronds reserved and roughly chopped
1 small head **chicory**, broken into leaves,
    any large leaves halved lengthways
freshly squeezed lemon juice
salt, for the cooking water

FOR THE DRESSING:
2 **anchovies in oil**, roughly chopped
2 heaped teaspoons **capers in brine**
1 clove of **garlic**, crushed
1 teaspoon **raw, unpasteurized apple
    cider vinegar** (with mother)
4 tablespoons **extra virgin olive oil**
2 tablespoons **Homemade Crème Fraîche**
    (see Tip, page 195) or **sour cream** (use
    vegan mayonnaise or **vegan crème
    fraiche** for DF)
1 teaspoon **freshly squeezed lemon juice**
freshly ground black pepper, to taste

Cooling potatoes changes their starchy interiors and increases their resistant starch, making them a better gut health option.

Bring a large pan of salted water to the boil and add the potatoes and the eggs. Set a timer for 7 minutes 30 seconds. When it goes off, remove the eggs with a slotted spoon and immediately plunge into a bowl of cold water. Leave to cool.

When the potatoes are cooked and tender to the point of a knife, after around 12 minutes, remove from the heat, drain, and leave to cool to room temperature.

When you are nearly ready to serve, prepare the fennel and chicory, place in a bowl, squeeze over a little lemon juice and gently toss (this helps stop them going brown).

Peel the eggs, and cut each into 6 wedges.

Use a stick blender or a small jug blender to whizz the dressing ingredients together. Taste. It should be tangy and creamy, and almost certainly won't need any salt.

Arrange the potatoes, fennel and chicory on a serving platter, in more or less a single layer. Then gently arrange the eggs on top. Drizzle over half the dressing, and serve with the remaining dressing alongside.

=TIP=

If you fancy some crunch, lightly toast some chopped hazelnuts or walnuts and add them along with the eggs.

SOBA NOODLE, TOFU & KIMCHI SOUP

SERVES 2

PREP TIME: 8 MINS * COOK TIME: 15 MINS

DF | V | NF

200g **soba noodles** (WF/GF if necessary)

500ml **hot water**

2 teaspoons **mirin** (or a pinch of **sugar**)

1 tablespoon **tamari/soy sauce**, or more, to taste (GF if needed)

1 head **pak choi**, stalks and leaves separated, large stalks chopped

2 **spring onions**, finely chopped

1 tablespoon **flavourless oil** (such as **rapeseed**)

2 **eggs**

100g **silken tofu**, drained and gently sliced into small cubes

100g **unpasteurized Kimchi** (see page 143), chopped

toasted sesame seeds, to garnish

Soba noodles are quick to cook and have a nuttier flavour than wheat-based noodles. We don't think there's anything wrong with wheat noodles, but good gut health is down to eating a wide variety of plant-based foods, and soba noodles are made with buckwheat – a seed – or a mixture of wheat and buckwheat.

Bring a pan of water to the boil, then plunge in the soba noodles and cook for 4½ minutes. Drain and rinse the noodles in cold water, then set aside.

To make the broth, pour the measured hot water into a large pan. Add the mirin (or sugar), then the tamari/soy sauce and bring up to a gentle simmer. Taste – you can add a little more tamari/soy sauce, if needed, but the kimchi will add salt later. Add the pak choi and spring onions and cook until the pak choi is just wilted, about 3 minutes.

Meanwhile, set a small frying pan over a medium heat and add the oil. When hot, crack in the eggs and fry until cooked to taste.

Divide the cooked soba noodles between 2 wide soup bowls. Add the cubed tofu. Divide the broth and pak choi between the bowls, then top each bowl with a fried egg.

Arrange the kimchi on top of the eggs and finish with a pinch of toasted sesame seeds. Eat immediately, breaking the yolk and stirring it into the broth.

≡TIP≡

If kimchi isn't your thing, hot sauce works instead.

GRAM FLOUR PASTA

SERVES 2

PREP TIME: 30 MINS PLUS RESTING TIME * COOK TIME: 2 MINS

DF | V | NF | SoF

150g **gram/chickpea flour**
50g **'00' pasta flour**, plus plenty
 for dusting
2 **whole eggs** and 1 **egg yolk**
1 tablespoon **extra virgin olive oil**
salt, for the cooking water

Gram or chickpea flour is higher in protein and fibre than traditional pasta flour, as well as being home to other micronutrients. You can make an entirely gluten-free pasta with it, but we find you get a better result with a little wheat flour. A pasta machine makes this a lot easier as the dough can be sticky.

Sift the flours into a large bowl. Make a well in the middle and add the eggs, yolk and olive oil. Use a wooden spoon to gradually work it into a craggy dough, then use your hands to bring it together. Flour a clean work surface and knead the dough for about 5 minutes, until smooth and springy. Set aside, in a bowl covered with a damp tea towel, for 1 hour.

Dust a large area of work surface and your hands with plenty of flour.

If you have a pasta machine, divide the rested dough into 4 pieces. Run each through several times on the lowest setting, folding the dough back on itself a couple of times, then run through on the next settings, until the dough is almost translucent, usually around the middle setting. If the lengths are becoming too long to handle, halve them. Lay them out on the floured work surface.

If you don't have a machine, cut the dough into 8 pieces and roll each out as thinly as possible, using lots of flour on the surface and rolling pin.

Cut the dough into long 5mm strips, either using the machine's cutting attachment or a sharp knife, to make tagliatelle (it's too sticky for spaghetti). Once cut, place on the floured surface in a single layer as the strands will still stick.

To cook, bring a large pan of well-salted water to the boil. Add the pasta and cook for just 2 minutes, then drain and serve immediately.

=TIP=

If you don't want to cook straight away, let the pasta dry a little until it no longer feels tacky but is still pliable. You can store it in a sealed container, loosely coiled, in the fridge for 2–3 days.

WALNUT & PARSLEY LINGUINE

SERVES 4

PREP TIME: 10 MINS ⋆ COOK TIME: 15 MINS

V | SoF

400g **linguine** (or similar chunky pasta)
3 tablespoons **olive oil**, for cooking
100g **walnuts**, chopped
1 tablespoon **pine nuts**
3 cloves of **garlic**, roughly chopped
1 small slice of **day-old bread**, crusts
    removed, torn into small pieces and
    soaked in a little **milk** (can be DF)
20g **Parmesan cheese**, finely grated, plus
    extra to serve (choose V/Ve, as needed)
2 tablespoons **full-fat Greek-style
    yoghurt** (or Ve/DF equivalent)
extra virgin olive oil, for drizzling
leaves from 3 or 4 sprigs of **fresh oregano**
    or **thyme** (optional)
sea salt and **freshly ground black pepper**

═TIP═

If you don't like the sound of
the rich nutty sauce, omit the
bread, milk and yoghurt and
simply toss everything else into
freshly cooked pasta.

The original northern Italian version of this Ligurian walnut sauce would be made with a hard-to-find tangy cheese. Here, Parmesan and yoghurt do a good job of replicating the flavour (a trick used by the late chef Antonio Carluccio, who grew up in neighbouring Piedmont).

Boil the pasta in a large pan of water for 1 minute less than the cooking instructions, or until al dente.

Heat the olive oil in a wide frying pan over a medium heat. Add the walnuts, pine nuts and garlic, and cook, stirring constantly, for 1–2 minutes until the nuts begin to brown – don't let the garlic burn. Remove from the heat and use tongs or a slotted spoon to set aside a generous handful of the walnuts. Tip the remaining mixture into a small blender or the jug of a stick blender. Squeeze the milk out of the soaked bread and add to the blender with the Parmesan, yoghurt and a pinch of salt. Blitz to a creamy, nutty sauce (it may look very thick at this point).

Drain the pasta, reserving a generous mugful of the cooking water. Return the pasta to the pan and drizzle over a little extra virgin olive oil. Toss.

Stir a few tablespoons of the cooking water into the sauce, adding more until you have a just-about pourable sauce. Taste, adding more salt or cheese as needed. Add the sauce to the pasta and toss to coat. If it looks too thick, stir in another tablespoon of the pasta water and toss again.

Divide between 4 plates or pasta bowls. Chop the reserved walnuts into small pieces and scatter over the pasta, along with a good dusting of grated Parmesan, the oregano or thyme leaves, if using, and some freshly ground black pepper.

PASTA E CECI

SERVES 4

PREP TIME: 25 MINS * COOK TIME: 30 MINS

V | NF | SoF

3 tablespoons **olive oil**

2 large **carrots**, finely diced

2 **onions**, finely diced

2 sticks **celery**, finely diced

2 cloves of **garlic**, finely chopped

1½ tablespoons finely chopped **red chilli** (optional)

2 tablespoons **tomato purée**

600–700ml **hot water**, plus extra as needed

1 tablespoon finely chopped **rosemary**

400g **canned chickpeas** in water, drained and rinsed (or 240g **cooked chickpeas**)

a generous pinch of **hot chilli flakes** or **mild red pepper flakes** (optional)

200g **small pasta tubes** (ditalini is traditional) (WF/GF if needed)

150g **kale** or other **dark green cabbage**, stems removed and finely sliced (optional)

salt and lots of **freshly ground black pepper**, to taste

freshly grated **Parmesan cheese** (V/Ve if needed), to serve

extra virgin olive oil, for drizzling

Pasta e ceci is an old recipe from Rome, and there are as many way to make it as there are cooks in the city. This is very loosely based on Rachel Roddy's version, although we add shredded greens in the last moments of cooking, which she would almost certainly not do.

Heat the oil in a large deep pan with a lid over a medium heat. Add the carrots, onions, celery and salt. Cook, stirring, until the vegetables are softened and the onion translucent but not browned, about 10 minutes. Add the garlic and chilli, if using, and cook for 2 minutes, stirring often. Add the tomato purée and cook, stirring, until it melds with the oil, which will turn a shimmering orange. Next, add 600ml hot water, plenty of black pepper, the rosemary, chickpeas and chilli/pepper flakes, if using. Bring to a simmer and cook for 5 minutes.

Optional: for a thicker, richer broth, remove about 2 ladlefuls of the stew and use a stick blender to blitz until completely smooth, then pour back into the pan.

Bring back to a simmer, then add the pasta. If the mixture looks really thick, add a splash more hot water. Cover with a lid and cook according to packet instructions, until the pasta is al dente, stirring now and then and topping up the water as needed.

If using, add the kale/cabbage 2 minutes before the pasta is done, stir and put the lid back on. (If you like well-cooked greens without any crunch, add 5 minutes before the pasta is cooked.)

When cooked, taste and add more seasoning (remember the cheese is salty, too) or chilli flakes, if you like. Serve in wide bowls, with Parmesan grated over and a drizzle of extra virgin olive oil.

═ TIP ═

Many Roman cooks –
including Rachel – would
melt in a couple of anchovies
at the beginning of cooking,
which not only adds umami,
but also a little hit of
omega-3.

PEA SHOOT & PISTACHIO PESTO

SERVES 4
PREP TIME: 5 MINS * COOK TIME: 5 MINS
WF | GF | DF | V | Ve | SoF

60g **pea shoots**
60g **basil leaves**
1 small clove of **garlic**
30g **shelled, roasted pistachios**
   (**salted** or **unsalted**)
4 tablespoons **extra virgin olive oil**
salt, as needed

TO SERVE (OPTIONAL):
Parmesan cheese (or V/Ve alternative)

A fresh pesto that just happens to be vegan.

Blitz all the ingredients together in a food processor to form a rough paste. Taste, adding salt only if you used unsalted pistachios – you shouldn't need any if they were salted.

Serve tossed through hot, freshly cooked pasta, with a little Parmesan grated over, if you like (we rather like it on its own, though).

=TIP=

Pesto is a great place to experiment with both nuts and leaves – try adding ground almonds or chopped hazelnuts, or using dill or tarragon.

VINCISGRASSI

SERVES 4-6

PREP TIME: 8 MINS * COOK TIME: 45–50 MINS

NF | SoF

olive oil, for greasing

500g **mushrooms** (we use a mixture of **chestnut** and **wild**)

knob of **butter** (or Ve/DF alternative), for cooking

a very big handful of **flat-leaf parsley leaves**, finely chopped

leaves from 3 sprigs of **thyme**, or 6 **sage leaves**, very finely chopped

75g **prosciutto** or Parma ham, torn into pieces (optional)

60ml **single cream** (optional)

8 **fresh egg lasagne sheets** (or dried egg-free sheets if Ve – follow the packet instructions)

about 75g **Parmesan chees**e (can be DF/V/Ve), finely grated

freshly ground black pepper

FOR THE BÉCHAMEL:

1 litre **milk** (can be DF)

½ **onion**

50g **butter** (or Ve/DF alternative)

50g **plain flour** (can be GF)

TO SERVE:

rocket and **sliced fennel** dressed with **lemon juice** and **extra virgin olive oil**

This rich, earthy lasagne is proof that gut-healthy food doesn't have to be raw or summery. Mushrooms have lots of fibre and, if you keep them on the windowsill to allow some sunlight exposure before cooking, they make extra vitamin D2, which is linked to good gut health. The ham is traditional but optional – make sure you season well if you leave it out.

Heat the oven to 200°C/400°F/gas mark 6. Grease a 30cm-long baking dish.

Sauté the mushrooms in batches in butter over a high heat until browned. Transfer to a large bowl and add the parsley, thyme or sage and ham, if using.

Meanwhile, start the béchamel. Warm the milk in a pan over a gentle heat and add the halved onion to infuse. Heat the butter in a large deep pan over a low heat. Once foaming, add the flour and stir to a golden paste. Add a little of the hot milk and stir briskly until incorporated. Continue adding milk, little by little, until you've added about half – going slow and steady prevents lumps. Add the rest in one go, but remove the onion first. Mix until smooth, then increase the heat and allow the sauce to thicken, stirring frequently. Remove from the heat.

Add the béchamel and cream, if using, to the mushrooms and mix well. Taste and season with pepper (remember the cheese is salty so you won't need extra salt).

Dip 2 lasagne sheets into a large bowl of freshly boiled water. Once pliable, remove with tongs and lay on the bottom of the baking dish. Add a third of the sauce and a layer of Parmesan. Repeat, finishing with a final layer of sauce and Parmesan.

Cook in the hot oven for 25 minutes, or until bubbling and light golden on top. Let stand for 5 minutes before serving with a robust, tart salad.

=TIP=

Love garlic? Add 3 cloves,
crushed, to the mushrooms
for the last minute of their
cooking time. You could also
replace the ham here with
cooked, chopped spinach, well
squeezed before adding.

CRISPY FRIED ALMOST-RAW VEGETABLES

SERVES 4

PREP TIME: 6-8 MINS * COOK TIME: 10–15 MINS

V | NF

350g **mixed vegetables**: **cauliflower florets**, **carrots**, **courgettes**, **long green beans**, **broccoli**, cut into batons or pieces of more or less the same size

plain flour (can be GF), for dredging

1–2 **eggs**, beaten

a splash of **milk**

100–150g **gluten-free** or **panko breadcrumbs**

flavourless vegetable oil (we like **rapeseed**), for cooking

for the kewpi-style mayo:

3 tablespoons good-quality **mayo** (can be Ve/NF/SoF)

1 teaspoon **soy sauce/tamari**, or more, to taste (can be GF)

TIP

If the crumbs are large – and GF crumbs in a packet are sometimes huge – pour them into a re-usable ziplock sandwich bag and give them a whack with a rolling pin until they look more crumb-like.

You can use regular panko breadcrumbs here, but we find gluten-free crumbs (usually rice-based) are best for shallow frying. The aim is to cook the vegetables really quickly, so that the breading crisps up before the vegetables have a chance to cook much at all. This makes quite a large amount, so halve the recipe if you just need a few pieces to top noodles or to serve as part of a larger spread.

Heat the oven to a low heat. Place a couple of tablespoons of flour into a bowl. Place 1 beaten egg in another bowl (save the other, as you may not need it) and stir in a splash of milk. Tip 100g of the breadcrumbs into a third bowl.

Set a wide frying pan over a medium heat. When hot, add enough oil to cover the base to a depth of about 5mm. Working briskly, dip the vegetable pieces into the flour first, then the egg, letting the excess drain away, and then the breadcrumbs. Be sure every piece is well covered in each layer of coating. Carefully place each piece into the hot oil. Cook for about 30 seconds–1 minute on each side, turning so that each side has a chance to crisp up and become golden in the hot oil. Remove from the pan using tongs and place on a plate lined with kitchen paper, to drain.

You will need to cook in batches, so keep the cooked pieces warm in the low oven. If you need more flour, egg or crumbs, top up the bowls as needed. Continue until all the vegetables are cooked.

Stir together the mayo and soy sauce.

Serve the vegetables while hot, with the kewpi-style mayo or other dipping sauces (hot sauce is good) on the side.

CAULIFLOWER FRITTERS

1 small **cauliflower** (350g), leaves and core trimmed (save the leaves for another dish, like **Slaw** on page 111)

½ teaspoon **fennel seeds**

1 teaspoon **cumin seeds**

½ teaspoon **mild red chilli flakes** (optional)

2 **eggs**, beaten

50g **plain flour** (can be GF)

½ teaspoon **baking powder**

125g **feta cheese**, crumbled

olive oil, for cooking

freshly ground black pepper

live plain yoghurt, to serve

TIP

These are ace with the addition of a couple of finely chopped spring onions, or a handful of chopped chives.

Rebecca has been making courgette and dill or carrot and cumin versions of these feta fritters for over a decade, but only recently realized cauliflower and feta might also be soul mates.

Heat the oven to a low heat.

Break or chop the cauliflower into small pieces, roughly 1cm. Place in a microwave-safe bowl with 4 tablespoons of water and zap on high for 3 minutes. Alternatively, blanch for 2 minutes in boiling water, then drain.

Meanwhile, toast the fennel and cumin seeds in a hot dry pan, just until they smell fragrant. Tip into a mixing bowl. Remove the cauliflower from the microwave, draining off any excess water, and add to the bowl along with the chilli flakes, if using, the beaten eggs, flour and baking powder. Mix thoroughly, then add the feta and some black pepper and mix again.

Place a wide frying pan over a medium heat. When hot, add enough olive oil to cover the base of the pan to a depth of about 5mm.

Use a dessertspoon to scoop the cauliflower mixture into the pan to make small fritters about 5cm across – any bigger and they will fall apart. Leave to cook until quite well set and golden on the bottom, as they will also fall apart if moved too quickly. Turn and cook the other side. If you can, turn each one onto its sides too, so they brown all over.

Keep the cooked fritters warm in the low oven while you cook the rest. Eat hot.

CRISPY SWEET POTATO FRITTERS

SERVES 2 AS A MAIN COURSE OR 4 AS A MEAL WITH OTHER DISHES
PREP TIME: 10 MINS, PLUS 30 MINS CHILLING ✳ COOK TIME: 40 MINS
DF | V | NF

700g **sweet potato**, peeled and cubed

1 tablespoon **white sesame seeds**
+ 1 tablespoon **black sesame seeds** (or one or other), toasted in a hot dry pan then roughly crushed

1 heaped tablespoon **miso paste** (or more to taste)

1 teaspoon **soy sauce/tamari** (can be GF)

3 **spring onions**, finely chopped, reserving a handful to garnish

50g **panko breadcrumbs** (or use WF/GF breadcrumbs)

2 **eggs**, beaten

plain flour, to coat (can be GF)

flavourless oil (rapeseed oil is good), for cooking

FOR THE SAUCE:

2 tablespoons **ketchup**

2 tablespoons **soy sauce/tamari** (can be GF)

½ teaspoon **miso paste**

FOR THE KEWPIE-STYLE MAYO:

2 tablespoons good-quality **mayonnaise** (can be Ve)

splash of **soy sauce/tamari** (can be GF), or to taste

This is inspired by a recipe for korroke in Tim Anderson's brilliant cookbook, 'Japaneasy'. Make into a main course with a slaw (see page 111), some Japanese-style pickles and some broccoli with Miso Butter (see page 126).

Simmer the potato in a large pan of water for about 15 minutes until tender. Drain and steam dry for a minute, then mash thoroughly, removing any fibrous lumps.

Mix half of the crushed sesame seeds into the mash, along with the miso, soy sauce/tamari and spring onions. Leave to cool, then chill in the fridge for 30 minutes to firm up.

When ready to cook, mix the remaining sesame seeds with the breadcrumbs in a small bowl. Place the beaten eggs in another bowl and a few tablespoons of flour on a plate. Heat the oven to a low heat.

Mix together the sauce ingredients and, separately, the mayo ingredients.

Pour 5mm of oil into a frying pan set over a medium heat. Scoop up a small ball of the sweet potato mixture and shape into a little patty. It will be quite soft and sticky, so smaller fritters will hold together better. Dip it into the flour, then the egg, coating thoroughly, then finally roll it in the sesame breadcrumbs. Place it carefully into the hot oil and cook for 3–4 minutes, until the bottom is a deep golden brown, crisp and firm. Flip and cook the other side.

Work in batches, wiping out the pan and adding fresh oil with each batch, otherwise the pan will fill with loose, burning breadcrumbs. Add more flour to the plate, as needed. Keep the cooked fritters warm in the oven. Serve hot, garnished with the reserved spring onions and the sauces for drizzling or dipping.

SPICY SQUASH WITH CREAMY POLENTA

SERVES 4

PREP TIME: X10 MINS * COOK TIME: 45–55 MINS

WF | GF | DF | V | Ve | NF | SoF

about 600g **butternut squash**, deseeded, skin on, cut into 3cm chunks (you can be flexible with quantities, if your squash is larger)

1 **red onion**, cut into 8 wedges

4 cloves of **garlic**, in their skins

a generous pinch of **hot** or **mild chilli flakes**, to taste (optional)

3 tablespoons **extra virgin olive oil**

1 tablespoon finely sliced **red chilli**

salt and **freshly ground black pepper**

extra virgin olive oil, to serve

FOR THE POLENTA:

150g **polenta**

450ml **boiling water**

150ml **milk** (can be DF/Ve/NF/SoF)

salt and **freshly ground black pepper**, to taste

TIP

Polenta is also excellent with pan-fried mushrooms and/or garlicky spinach or kale on top.

Squash, especially the skin, is high in fibre. Cooking with the skin on is nutritious, and it helps the squash to roast without becoming squishy, and it tastes good, too. Although the polenta will set if chilled, leftovers can be eaten at room temperature or given a blast in the microwave.

Check the packet for when to start cooking the polenta. Quick-cook polenta will cook in just a few minutes, whereas traditional polenta can take up to 45 minutes.

Heat the oven to 180°C/350°F/gas mark 4.

Use 1 large or 2 smaller roasting trays. Toss together the squash, onion, garlic, chilli flakes, if using, olive oil and some black pepper. Spread out in a single layer in the tray(s) and roast in the oven for 30 minutes.

Add the sliced chilli and toss again. Increase the heat to 200°C/400°F/gas mark 6 and cook for a further 25 minutes, or until the onion is browning and the squash tender (check after 15 minutes). Remove from the oven, take out the garlic and set aside. Season the roasted veg with a little salt and keep warm.

Meanwhile, cook the polenta. Bring the water and milk to a simmer in a deep pan. Pour in the polenta in a slow stream, stirring all the time to stop lumps forming. Reduce the heat and cook according to the packet instructions, stirring often. If the polenta gets too thick, add a little water or milk – it should be soft, creamy and not at all gritty. Season to taste with salt and pepper.

Pop the roasted garlic from their skins, mash to a paste with the flat side of a knife, then stir into the polenta. Serve the spicy squash and onions on top of the polenta, finishing with a little drizzle of extra virgin olive oil.

ARTICHOKES WITH GARLIC, ALMONDS & ANCHOVIES

SERVES 2 WITH PASTA OR 4 AS A SIDE
PREP TIME: 6 MINS ★ COOK TIME: 25 MINS
WF | GF | DF | SoF

2 tablespoons **olive oil**

1 large **onion**, finely sliced

3 **anchovies**

2 cloves of **garlic**, crushed

3 tablespoons **flaked almonds**

400g **canned artichokes** in water, drained (240g drained weight), then rinsed and cut into quarters

a drizzle of **extra virgin olive oil**

salt and **freshly ground black pepper**, to taste

freshly squeezed lemon juice, to taste

This is inspired by a traditional Sicilian dish (although we are pretty sure no Sicilian would ever make it with canned artichokes). Treat it as a side with grilled fish or lamb chops, or toss into freshly cooked pasta with some Parmesan cheese.

Pour 1 tablespoon of the oil into a wide, deep pan set over a low–medium heat and add the onion. Cook really slowly, stirring often, until it begins to caramelize, but don't let it burn as it will taste bitter. This step can't be rushed and might take 15 minutes or so – if it cooks too fast, turn the heat down.

Once the onions are sticky-looking and jammy, add the anchovies and the remaining tablespoon of oil. Let the anchovies cook down and melt into the onions for a couple of minutes, stirring a couple of times. When they've disappeared into the mixture, add the garlic and almonds and increase the heat a little. Let the almonds toast slightly in the hot, garlicky oil, but don't let them burn. Finally, add the quartered artichokes and cook just long enough to heat through, stirring, for 3–4 minutes.

Just before serving, add a drizzle of extra virgin olive oil, some salt and pepper and a squeeze of lemon juice, to taste.

Eat hot, warm or at room temperature.

═TIP═

If you're feeling fancy, use grilled artichokes in olive oil (not brine) from a jar.

COCONUT, JACKFRUIT & LIME CURRY

SERVES 4

PREP TIME: 15 MINS ★ COOK TIME: 35–40 MINS

WF | GF | DF | V | Ve | NF | SoF

1 tablespoon **extra virgin olive oil**

1 small **onion**, finely chopped

1 small **carrot**, finely chopped

1 clove of **garlic**, crushed

2 teaspoons **mild curry powder**

400ml **full-fat coconut milk**

200ml **chicken** or **vegetable stock**

400g **sweet potato**, peeled and diced into 2cm chunks

a tiny pinch of **dried thyme**

a pinch of **ground allspice**

1 tablespoon finely chopped **red chilli**, seeds removed or not, to taste

400g **canned young green jackfruit** in water, drained

50g **kale**, ribs removed, finely shredded

juice of ½ **lime**

salt, to taste (optional)

steamed brown rice, to serve

This is inspired by the new jackfruit curry we added to the LEON menu in 2020.

Set a deep, wide pan with a lid over a medium heat. When hot, add the oil and then the onion and carrot. Cook for about 10 minutes, stirring often, until soft but not browned. Add the garlic and curry powder and cook, stirring, for 1 minute. Add the coconut milk, stock and sweet potato, bring up to a simmer, then add the thyme, allspice and red chilli.

Once everything is in the pan, shred the drained jackfruit chunks, using your hands to pull it apart and removing any tough woody parts and seeds that you find. Add the shredded jackfruit to the pan and bring back to a simmer, then cover with a lid and cook for 15–20 minutes, until the sweet potato is tender but not mushy or collapsing. For the last couple of minutes of cooking, add the shredded kale.

Remove from the heat. Just before serving, squeeze over a little lime juice, then taste and add salt, if needed. Serve alongside steamed brown rice.

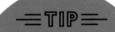

≡TIP≡

You can buy ready-shredded jackfruit, if you find that easier. We tend to buy it in cans as they're simpler to recycle and cheaper.

KALE, PAK CHOI & BROCCOLI WITH GARLIC FRIED RICE

SERVES 4

PREP TIME: 10 MINS * COOK TIME: 10 MINS

WF | GF | DF | V | Ve | NF

1 large head **garlic**, cloves peeled and finely chopped (pulse in a food processor to save time and garlicky fingers)

3 tablespoons **vegetable oil**

8–10 **spring onions**, light green and white parts thinly sliced, green parts thinly sliced and reserved to serve

100g **kale**, ribs removed, roughly chopped

100g **tenderstem broccoli**, sliced into even-sized batons

1 **pak choi**, thick stems removed, sliced the same size as the broccoli

800g **chilled day-old rice** (start with 265g uncooked rice)

1 tablespoon **soy sauce/tamari** (choose GF if needed)

1 tablespoon **dark soy sauce/tamari** (choose GF if needed)

1 teaspoon **sugar**

salt

TO SERVE:

sesame oil

1 **lime**, cut into wedges

Sriracha (optional, but encouraged)

Fried rice is a stir-fry standby that never fails to disappoint. This version uses crispy garlic and fries everything else in the garlic-infused oil.

Intriguingly, the carbs in rice (and potatoes) change when they are cooked and cooled, turning into resistant starch – the kind our gut microbes love. Always cool cooked rice quickly, transferring it to the fridge as soon as possible, or less-friendly microbes may colonize it.

To make the crispy garlic, lightly season the chopped garlic with salt. In a small pan, heat the oil over a medium heat. Add the garlic and fry until very slightly browned and crispy, 2–3 minutes. The garlic should be gently bubbling, not spitting – reduce the heat if needed. Keep watch as the garlic can easily burn and turn bitter. Once the garlic is crispy, drain immediately, reserving the oil. Transfer the garlic to a plate lined with kitchen paper, to cool.

Heat 1 tablespoon of the garlic oil in a large wok or frying pan over a high heat. When smoking hot, add the spring onions, kale, broccoli and pak choi. Season lightly with salt. Stir fry, tossing constantly, until softened and fragrant, 2–3 minutes. Add more garlic oil as needed to prevent sticking. Transfer to a plate.

Add another tablespoon of garlic oil to the same pan. Add the rice and break up any clumps with a wooden spoon. Stir fry until the rice is broken up and softened, 1–2 minutes. Return the vegetables to the pan and add the soy sauce/tamari, dark soy sauce/tamari and sugar. Toss to combine and fry for a further minute.

Divide between 4 bowls and top generously with crispy garlic and sliced spring onion greens. Serve with a drizzle of sesame oil, lime wedges and Sriracha.

≡TIP≡

In season, make this more, well... rainbowy by using rainbow chard instead of the kale.

CAULIFLOWER RICE CHICKEN BIRYANI

SERVES 4 WITH OTHER DISHES

PREP TIME: 15 MINS PLUS 30 MINS TO MARINATE * COOK TIME: 30 MINS

WF | GF | SoF

400g **boneless chicken thighs**, cut into 4–5cm chunks

4 tablespoons **extra virgin olive oil** or melted **ghee**

2 **onions**, finely sliced

1 **cauliflower** (about 700g), trimmed and broken into florets

seeds from 2 **cardamom pods**

a pinch of **fennel seeds**

a dusting of freshly grated **nutmeg**

½ teaspoon **garam masala**

½ teaspoon **ground turmeric**

a pinch of **ground cloves**

a pinch of **cumin seeds**

a pinch of **saffron**, crumbled

2 tablespoons **raisins** or **sultanas**

3 tablespoons **flaked almonds**

a handful of **coriander leaves**

a knob of **butter/ghee**

freshly squeezed lemon juice

FOR THE MARINADE:

2 tablespoons **plain yoghurt** (can be DF)

2cm piece of **ginger**, peeled and finely grated

1 clove of **garlic**, crushed

1 teaspoon **garam masala**

½ teaspoon **ground turmeric**

a pinch of **salt**

We're delighted with this cauliflower 'rice' biryani – the cauliflower takes on all those lovely, gentle spice flavours and cooks briefly in the pan while the chicken finishes. Delicious with dhal on the side.

Mix together the marinade ingredients. Add the chicken to the marinade, stirring to coat. Marinate in the fridge for at least 30 minutes and up to 24 hours.

Heat 2 tablespoons of the oil in a frying pan over a low–medium heat. Add the onions and gently cook, stirring, for about 20 minutes until golden brown.

Working in batches, blitz the cauliflower florets to 'rice' in a food processor and place in a large bowl. Grind the cardamom seeds to a powder in a pestle and mortar and mix into the cauliflower along with the other spices, raisins, half of the almonds and 1 tablespoon of the oil.

Heat the final tablespoon of ghee/oil in a large, heavy-based deep pan with a lid over a medium–high heat. Add the chicken, in batches if necessary, and cook for about 8 minutes until slightly browned. Remove the chicken and scrape any burnt bits off the pan. Return the chicken to the pan, along with any juices, and arrange in a single layer. Top with half of the cauliflower, then arrange half of the fried onions and the coriander in a layer on top. Finish with another layer of cauliflower, the rest of the onions and almonds. Drizzle over 3 tablespoons of water and dot the top with the butter/ghee. Cover with the lid and place over a low heat for 10 minutes.

Taste. We like our 'rice' to have a little bite, but if you prefer it softer, remove from the heat, recover with the lid and leave to steam for another 2 minutes. Squeeze over a little lemon juice before serving.

=TIP=

For a vegan version, swap
the chicken for chunks
of cooked sweet potato,
green beans and a
handful of peas (and use
vegan yoghurt and ghee).

RINKU'S PANCHRATAN 5-PULSE DHAL

60g **red split lentils** (masoor dal)

60g **Bengal gram/split chickpeas** (chana dal)

60g **split pigeon peas** (toor dal)

60g **black lentils** (urad dal)

60g **small whole green gram lentils** (moong dal)

750ml **cold water**

2 large **tomatoes**, chopped

3 cloves of **garlic**, finely chopped

1 teaspoon **ground turmeric**

2 tablespoon **ghee** or **rapeseed oil** (use oil or vegan ghee if Ve or DF)

1 **bay leaf**

2 **green chillies**, slit lengthways

2 teaspoons **cumin seeds**

2 **white onions**, finely chopped

1 tablespoon grated **fresh ginger**

¼ teaspoon **asafoetida**

1 teaspoon **salt**

coriander leaves, to garnish

'This is my version of a Mughlai dhal,' says our go-to Happy dhal expert Rinku Dutt, who runs Raastawala, a Calcutta-inspired food business in London. 'The secret is that the longer the lentils are cooked, the creamier the dish becomes, without the need for cream.' This has loads of fibre and prebiotics. Eat with chapattis or steamed basmati rice and a simple cucumber salad.

Place all the lentils in a heavy-based pan and rinse thoroughly with cold water 2–3 times, until the water is only very slightly cloudy. Drain.

Cover the lentils with the measured cold water and bring to the boil over a medium heat. Skim off and discard the white foam that forms on top of the water. Mix in half the tomatoes and half the garlic, along with the turmeric, and bring to the boil again. After 5 minutes, reduce the heat to low and place a lid on the pan. Simmer for 20–25 minutes, stirring occasionally, until the lentils soften and meld together (some lentils may need to simmer for longer).

Heat the ghee or oil in a small pan over a medium heat. Add the bay leaf, chillies and cumin seeds. Cook until the aromas are released, but take care not to burn the seeds. Stir in the onions and cook, stirring often, until the onions are translucent, then add the remaining tomatoes and garlic, and the ginger. Continue cooking this 'temper' mixture until it begins to look glossy.

Once the temper is ready and the dhal is slightly thickened and creamy, remove the lid, increase the heat to medium and bring to a simmer. Add the asafoetida and half of the salt, and stir in well. Taste, adding the rest of the salt if needed. Carefully add the hot temper mixture to the dhal, stir and leave to simmer for another 3 minutes. Garnish with coriander and serve.

═TIP═

Swap in other lentils if you don't have the ones listed – green lentils, French lentils, brown lentils and split black gram all work (but avoid whole beans and chickpeas).

ZAKKOKU MAI

SERVES 4

PREP TIME: 5 MINS ★ COOK TIME: 26 MINS

WF | GF | DF | V | Ve | SoF

200g **uncooked Japanese white rice**

1 tablespoon **uncooked buckwheat**

1 tablespoon **uncooked quinoa**

1 tablespoon **uncooked freekeh** (omit if WF/GF)

1 tablespoon **uncooked bulgur wheat** (omit if WF/GF)

1 tablespoon **uncooked millet grain**

1 tablespoon **uncooked amaranth seeds**

1 tablespoon **ground flaxseeds**

1 tablespoon **toasted sesame seeds** (black, white or a mixture)

a pinch of **salt**

This Japanese recipe was once a staple food, especially in mountainous regions. Now, because it contains so many useful nutrients and much more fibre than white rice, it has become popular again. Zakkoku rice involves cooking wholegrains and seeds in the same pan as the rice – and you can tailor it to your needs (and to use up whatever you have in the cupboard). Some versions even contain oats. Just stick to the rough ratio below – 8 parts rice to 3 parts grains and seeds.

Although we make zakkoku mai with Japanese rice – to serve with dishes like the Miso-Crusted Salmon on page 174 – you can also make it with brown rice or wild rice to match whatever you're cooking.

Stir the rice and all the grains together. If you have a fine sieve, it's a good idea to give the whole lot a rinse before cooking.

This mixture should be 200ml by volume, so should need 300ml of cold water for cooking. If you are making more zakkoku rice, then measure the volume of the mixture and use 1½ times its volume of water.

Place the rice and water in a pan with a lid. Bring to the boil, cover with the lid and simmer for 16 minutes, stirring once at the beginning and a couple of times again towards the end, so that the mixture doesn't stick and burn.

Remove from the heat. Fluff the grains up with a fork, then cover and leave to stand for at least 10 minutes.

TIP

Make a larger batch of zakkoku and store (uncooked!) in a jar, ready for later use. Freekeh and quinoa add their own flavours to cooked zakkoku mai, and can be bitter, so leave out if you don't enjoy them.

BIBIMBAP WITH MARINATED BEEF & VEGETABLES

SERVES 4

PREP TIME: 15 MINS * COOK TIME: 45 MINS

DF | NF

500g **grass-fed beef sirloin** or **rump steak**, thinly sliced

4 tablespoons **vegetable oil**

12–15 **fresh shiitake mushrooms**, thinly sliced

2 cloves of **garlic**, minced

200g **baby spinach**

1 large **carrot**, cut into small matchsticks

50g **beansprouts**

salt, to taste

FOR THE RICE:

400g **brown rice**, well rinsed

800ml **water**

2 tablespoons **coconut oil**

1 tablespoon **soy sauce**

FOR THE BEEF MARINADE:

½ **green apple**, grated

2 cloves of **garlic**, grated

1 tablespoon **soy sauce**

1 tablespoon **honey**

1 tablespoon **toasted sesame oil**

2 teaspoons **rice vinegar**

Bibimbap is a well-known Korean dish of rice and a variety of deliciously sauced toppings and this is our homage to it. It sounds fiddly to prepare because everything needs to be cooked individually, but don't worry. You can do it all in the time the rice takes to cook – get two pans going if you're feeling confident. The vegetables are traditionally served at room temperature so there's no need to rush. Just make sure you cook the beef and egg at the last minute so they are piping hot.

For the rice: Combine all the ingredients in a pan and bring to the boil. Cover, reduce the heat and simmer for 45 minutes. Remove from the heat and leave to stand, covered, for 10 minutes. Fluff with a fork.

Whisk together the beef marinade ingredients in a large bowl. Add the beef and mix thoroughly. Leave for 30 minutes.

In a small bowl, stir the bibimbap sauce ingredients together until smooth.

Heat 1 tablespoon of the vegetable oil in a large pan over a medium–high heat. Add the mushrooms and stir-fry for 3–4 minutes. Add the garlic and fry for a further 1–2 minutes. Season lightly with salt and transfer to a plate.

Heat a further tablespoon of the oil in the same pan. Add the spinach and sauté until wilted, 1–2 minutes. Season lightly with salt and transfer to a plate. Squeeze out any excess moisture when cooled slightly.

Heat another tablespoon of the oil in the same pan. Add the carrots and cook until just tender, 2–3 minutes. You want the carrots to still have some bite.

FOR THE BIBIMBAP SAUCE:
2 tablespoons **gochujang**
1 tablespoon **honey**
1 tablespoon **toasted sesame oil**
1 tablespoon **rice vinegar**
1 tablespoon **water**
1 teaspoon **soy sauce**
1 clove of **garlic**, grated

TO SERVE:
4 **eggs**
greens of 4 **spring onions**, thinly sliced
toasted sesame seeds (black or white)
toasted sesame oil
1 **lime**, cut into wedges
Sriracha (optional, but a great idea)

Simmer the beansprouts in a separate pan of boiling water for 4 minutes until tender. Drain and rinse under cold water. Squeeze out excess water.

Just before you are ready to serve, heat the final 1 tablespoon of oil in a large wok or frying pan over a high heat. Add the beef and stir-fry for 3–4 minutes until cooked through and bits have caramelized and stuck to the pan. Transfer to a plate. Fry the eggs in the same pan to your preferred level of doneness (we like a runny yolk).

To assemble: divide the rice between 4 bowls, then top with the vegetables and beef. Spoon over some of the sauce. Top each with a fried egg, scatter over the spring onions and sesame seeds and drizzle over a bit of sesame oil. Serve with lime wedges and Sriracha.

≡TIP≡

We use grass-fed beef because it is relatively rich in omega-3, but you can use chicken, tofu, or just vegetables. Anything is going to taste good mixed in with that sauce.

RYE CRACKERS

MAKES ABOUT 40 CRACKERS

PREP TIME: 5 MINS PLUS PROVING TIME * COOK TIME: 15 MINS

V | NF | SoF

50g **rye flour**, plus extra for dusting
100g **plain flour**
85ml **water**
1 tablespoon **full-fat live plain yoghurt**
3 tablespoons **olive oil**
pinch of **fine salt**

These rye crackers are very moreish and a great vehicle for a bit of (unpasteurised) cheese.

In a bowl, mix all the ingredients together, first with a spoon, and then using your hands to knead the dough into a neat ball. Wrap in clingfilm or cover with a clean, damp tea towel and set aside for about 1 hour.

When ready to cook, heat the oven to 200°C/400°F/gas mark 6. Line 2 or more baking sheets with baking paper.

Flour a clean work surface and rolling pin. Unwrap the dough and divide into 3 pieces. Roll out each piece until about 2mm thick, then cut into whatever shape you like – we go for triangles as they work well for dipping. Arrange the shapes on the baking sheets as you go.

Bake in the oven for 7 minutes, or until crisp.

Remove and allow to cool. Eat immediately. Alternatively, when completely cool, store in a sealed container and eat within 3 days.

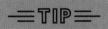

TIP

Depending on what you plan to serve these with, add some seeds or flavourings: poppy seeds, caraway seeds, sesame seeds, freshly grated Parmesan cheese or just some flaky salt and black pepper. Whatever you choose, press the ingredients lightly into the uncooked dough, or they will fall off after cooking.

CANNELLINI BEAN MASH

120ml **extra virgin olive oil**

4 cloves of **garlic**, roughly chopped into chunks

2 small sprigs of **rosemary**

800g **canned cannellini beans** in water, drained but not rinsed

zest of ¼ **unwaxed lemon** and about 1 teaspoon of **lemon juice**, to taste

sea salt and **freshly ground black pepper**

For such humble ingredients, this mash tastes luxurious, and works beautifully with lamb chops and wilted greens, or sautéed mushrooms, or slathered onto hot toast with a spoonful of ricotta, some red chilli and a drizzle of olive oil. Yes, it does contain quite a lot of olive oil. No, we're not sorry. Just think of those lovely polyphenols and how happy your microbes will be.

Pour the oil into a frying pan set over a low-medium heat. When hot, add the garlic, a small pinch of salt and the rosemary sprigs. Cook for 3–4 minutes, until the rosemary looks frazzled and the garlic is golden but definitely not browned or burnt (as then it will be bitter). Use a slotted spoon to lift both the garlic and rosemary out of the oil and set aside to cool.

Carefully tip the beans into the pan (watch out for splattering from the oil), along with any gloopy cooking liquid still clinging to the cans, and stir. Once piping hot, after a couple of minutes, remove from the heat. Finely chop the cooled garlic and add back to the pan, then carefully mash the beans and garlic together using a potato masher. Alternatively, if you prefer posh mash or don't like the idea of it being chunky, blitz it with a blender until smooth. Once roughly mashed, add the lemon zest and juice and mix again. Taste and add a little salt and lots of pepper, and more lemon juice if needed.

Serve immediately, with the fried rosemary needles crumbled over the top, or chill in the fridge and bring up to room temperature, or reheat, before eating.

≡TIP≡

Surprisingly, this really benefits from a couple of tablespoonfuls of full-fat plain, live yoghurt – the creamy tang works with the mellowness of the beans, especially if you're using this to top toast, with a sprinkle of chopped fresh dill.

≡TIP≡

Another dressing option:
omit the anchovy and add
a couple of tablespoons of
well-crumbled blue cheese
instead – mash/mix until
completely smooth.

CHARRED GEM LETTUCE

SERVES 2 AS A LIGHT MAIN, 4 AS A SIDE OR STARTER
PREP TIME: 12 MINS * COOK TIME: 12 MINS
WF | GF

2 **little gem lettuces**, or 1 **large romaine/
cos lettuce**
olive oil, for cooking
salt and **freshly ground black pepper**,
to taste

FOR THE DRESSING:
3 tablespoons **unsweetened milk kefir**
(store-bought or homemade, see page
155) or **full-fat plain live yoghurt** (can
be DF), **sour cream** or **crème fraîche**
2 teaspoons finely chopped **flat-leaf
parsley**
1 teaspoon **extra virgin olive oil**
a pinch of zest from an **unwaxed lemon**
½ teaspoon **lemon juice**
¼ teaspoon **Dijon mustard**
1 teaspoon finely chopped **chives**
1 **anchovy in oil**, very finely chopped and
then smooshed to a paste
2 teaspoons good-quality **mayonnaise**
salt and **freshly ground black pepper**,
to taste

FOR THE NUTS:
20g **blanched hazelnuts**, roughly chopped
1 teaspoon **salted butter**
1 teaspoon **honey**

If you haven't tried char-cooking lettuce, you're in for a treat – the lettuces brown on their cut sides and stay firm and crunchy on the insides. (This also works on a barbecue, once the flames have completely died down and the coals are white.)

This Caesar-ish dressing is a great way to work kefir into your cooking, if you've got some fermenting in the fridge, but yoghurt, sour cream or crème fraîche will also do the trick. In fact, a straightforward lemon and extra virgin olive oil dressing (see page 170) works perfectly, too.

Mix all the dressing ingredients together until smooth, then taste and add more seasoning or lemon, as needed. Set aside until ready to serve.

Next, make the nuts. Place the nuts, butter and honey into a small frying pan set over a low-medium heat and cook, stirring, until the nuts are coated and are just turning golden. Remove from the heat and tip into a small bowl (left in the pan, they will burn). Set aside.

Cut each lettuce into quarters, lengthways, leaving as much of the base intact as you can – this will stop the outer leaves falling off and into the pan.

Set a frying pan over a fairly high heat and add a splash of olive oil. When hot, place the lettuce wedges into the pan, cut-side down. Cook for a couple of minutes, just until the cut side begins to char, then turn and cook the other cut sides. Remove from the heat and season with a little salt and pepper, then arrange on serving plates or one big platter. Drizzle over the dressing and top with the honeyed nuts. Serve immediately.

HERBED FREEKEH

250g **ready-cooked freekeh** (or simmer 80g **uncooked cracked** or **whole freekeh** in water or stock as noted opposite)

leaves from 2 sprigs of **mint**, finely chopped

2 tablespoons finely chopped **fresh dill**

a really generous handful of **flat-leaf parsley leaves**, roughly chopped

1 tablespoon finely chopped **coriander leaves** (optional)

1 small stick of **celery**, very finely diced (dice and add any **celery leaves**, too)

a pinch of zest from an **unwaxed lemon**

FOR THE DRESSING:

1 tablespoon **freshly squeezed lemon juice**

2 tablespoons **extra virgin olive oil**

½ teaspoon **pomegranate molasses** (or add a pinch of **brown sugar**)

¼ teaspoon **ground cumin**, or more to taste

salt, to taste

Freekeh is made from young green wheat, which is then roasted to give it a subtly smoky flavour, and can be used in place of bulgur or couscous. Simmered in water or stock, cracked freekeh cooks more quickly (15–20 minutes) than whole (45–50 minutes). Alternatively, you can buy it ready-cooked. It's high in fibre with naturally-occurring prebiotics, and very tasty. Treat this as a base for a Rainbow Salad (see page 86) or serve as a side to things like a summery roast chicken or roasted aubergine.

Mix all the salad ingredients together in a large serving bowl.

Stir together the dressing ingredients, then taste and adjust the seasoning and cumin levels, if you like. Tip the whole lot over the salad. Toss, then taste and adjust the seasoning again, if needed.

=TIP=

To turn this into a main course, add cooked peas, pistachio nuts and pomegranate seeds, and top with crumbled feta cheese.

RADISH, POTATO & DILL SALAD

SERVES 4 AS A SALAD WITH OTHER DISHES
PREP TIME: 10 MINS ★ COOK TIME: 12 MINS
WF | GF | V | SoF

250g **new potatoes**, halved

75g **radishes**, cut into wedges (if they happen to have fresh-looking greens attached, roughly chop them and add to the salad)

75g **cucumber**, cut into small chunks

2–3 tablespoons **thick full-fat plain live yoghurt** (or use an unsweetened non-dairy live yoghurt if DF or Ve)

1 tablespoon finely chopped **fresh dill**

1 teaspoon finely chopped **fresh chives** or finely chopped **spring onion greens** (both optional)

1 teaspoon good-quality **extra virgin olive oil**

salt and **freshly ground black pepper**

A fresher, crunchier take on the classic potato salad. Potatoes form resistant starch as they cool, which our microbes love.

Cook the potatoes in boiling water for 12 minutes, or until tender to the point of a knife. Allow to cool.

Place all the ingredients in a large bowl, starting with just 2 tablespoons of the yoghurt and adding the third only if needed. Stir well and taste to check the seasoning.

Serve immediately, although leftovers will keep, covered in the fridge, for 1–2 days. If chilled, remove from the fridge about 30 minutes before serving, to re-awaken the flavours.

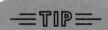

=TIP=

Make a meal of this by adding some chunks of hot-smoked fish (trout or mackerel), a big handful of peppery watercress and maybe a sliced, soft-yolked but hard-boiled egg (cook a room-temperature egg in boiling water for 7 minutes 30 seconds, cool in cold water, then peel).

PICKLED SHIITAKE

SERVES 1 × 400ML JAR

PREP TIME: 5 MINS PLUS 20 MINS SOAKING * COOK TIME: 20 MINS

WF | GF | DF | V | Ve

50g **dried shiitake mushrooms**

3cm piece of **fresh ginger**, cut into thin slices

100ml **soy sauce/tamari** (choose GF if needed)

100ml **rice vinegar**

4 tablespoons **sugar**

This one is all about getting more delicious 'shroomy fibre into our diets, since a) it's not a true fermented pickle, and b) boiling it kills any good bacteria. But that's okay, because c) it's unbelievably delicious. Inspired by the pickled shiitake served in Momofuku, NYC.

Place the dried mushrooms in a bowl and cover with at least 100ml boiling water. Set aside to rehydrate for 15–20 minutes.

Place the ginger, soy sauce/tamari, vinegar and sugar in a pan with a lid. Drain the mushrooms, reserving 100ml of the soaking liquid and add it to the pan along with the mushrooms. Bring the mixture to a simmer and cook for 20 minutes. Remove from the heat, fish out the ginger and pour into a jar or tub with a lid. Allow to cool, then place in the fridge. These will keep in a sealed container in the fridge for several weeks.

TIP

These are best served cold, as a side to Japanese-style dishes (like the Miso-Crusted Salmon on page 174), but you can also serve them on top of noodles or noodle soup dishes.

EAT THE RAINBOW

Eating a rainbow of plant-based foods gives our good gut bacteria the range of nutrients they need to thrive.

CORN CAKES WITH POACHED EGGS & SPICY ROAST TOMATOES

SERVES 2

PREP TIME: 15 MINS * COOK TIME: 20–25 MINS

WF | GF | DF | V | NF

2–4 **eggs**

a squeeze of **lemon juice**

a handful of **herbs**: **chives**, **parsley**, **coriander**, **dill** or a mixture, finely chopped

FOR THE TOMATOES:

200g **cherry tomatoes**, halved

½ **red chilli**, deseeded and finely chopped (or more or less, to taste)

¼ teaspoon **nigella seeds**

¼ teaspoon **mustard seeds**

a pinch of **cumin seeds**

a splash of **flavourless oil**

2 cloves of **garlic**, crushed (optional)

3cm piece of **ginger**, peeled and grated

a pinch of **sugar**

½ teaspoon **raw, unpasteurized apple cider vinegar** (with mother)

FOR THE CORN CAKES:

200g **frozen sweetcorn**

6 tablespoons **gram/chickpea flour**

2 **spring onions**, finely chopped (optional)

4 tablespoons **water**

a splash of **flavourless oil**

salt and **freshly ground black pepper**

These vegan, gluten-free corn cakes are really versatile and they're also great for kids. Make a big batch, then freeze the uncooked corn cakes.

Heat the oven to 180°C/350°F/gas mark 4. Combine the tomatoes, chilli and spices in a roasting tray with a splash of oil, stir to coat, then arrange in a single layer. Roast in the oven for 8 minutes, then remove and add the garlic (if using), ginger and sugar. Stir again and return to the oven for 8 minutes. Keep watch so the garlic doesn't burn. Remove when the tomatoes are softened, allow to cool slightly, then stir through the apple cider vinegar (use less if it's very tart).

Meanwhile, add the sweetcorn to a pan of boiling water and bring back to the boil. Drain and tip into a food processor with the flour, spring onions and water. Blitz to roughly purée, keeping some sweetcorn whole. Season with salt and pepper to taste.

Heat a splash of oil in a large frying pan over a medium heat. When hot, use a spoon to scoop 6 sweetcorn patties into the pan, each about 6cm in diameter (you may need to cook in batches). Cook fairly slowly so that the middles set and the bottoms turn a rich golden brown. Use 2 spatulas to turn the patties as they will be fragile. Cook until the other sides are brown and the patties have firmed up. If cooking in batches, keep the first batch warm in the oven while you cook the rest.

Poach the eggs in a pan of boiling water to which you've added a squeeze of lemon juice. When done to your liking, remove, drain and pat dry with kitchen paper.

Serve the corn cakes topped with the eggs, tomatoes and herbs. Eat immediately.

=TIP=

If you don't fancy the spice, simply roast the tomatoes in oil with some salt and pepper. If you don't do eggs, just leave them out. And if your tummy struggles with legumes, swap the chickpea flour for 2 eggs and 2–3 tablespoons plain flour, adding water just 1 tablespoon at a time, until the batter is thick and spoonable.

HOW TO BUILD A RAINBOW SALAD

We've been making and serving salads for a long time – in fact, our very first Happy book was 'Happy Salads'. Salads mean a lot to us and we love experimenting with them.

Consider this a guide. Salads can handle a bit of inventiveness and, with the right additions, can work perfectly as a main course. The idea behind creating a rainbow salad is, obviously, to get plenty of colourful ingredients into our diets – but it has to taste good, too. Don't go absolutely crazy – using too many ingredients will lead to an overwhelming messy mulch.

Think about pairings. Some are deliciously contrasting, such as sweet with salty (feta with roasted squash), or sour with creamy (cranberries with Brie), while others match each other, like tangy lemon zest in a yoghurt dressing. Which does your salad need?

THE BASE

This could Herbed Freekeh (page 76), Pomegranate & Pistachio Quinoa (page 116), Sour Thai-style Salad (page 91), or plain wholegrain couscous, quinoa or freekeh.

THE ARCHITECTURE

This could be leaves or raw vegetables, such as fennel or cucumber; cooled steamed potatoes; or leftover roasted root veg – aubergine or courgette. Choose one or two ingredients with simple flavours to fill out the salad. Ideally they should also introduce some colour – pink slivers of beetroot, orange twists of carrot, yellow ribbons of summer squash. Depending on the rest of the salad, this colour could also come from fruit: apple, pear, melon, grapes, orange, papaya and even mango can work.

THE INTEREST

Often, the interest is protein-based, but it's about flavour, too. This could be sharp crumbly cheese, smoked tofu, roasted chickpeas, cooked seafood, cured fish, nuggets of fried halloumi, charcuterie, soft-boiled eggs, a ball of creamy mozzarella, tuna in olive oil…

THE TEXTURE

If your vegetables bring this, then you might not need more, but a good rainbow salad has crunch. Try roasted walnuts or hazelnuts, popped seeds or grains, or peanuts if you're making something to go with Asian-style food. Try crisping up big crumbs of sourdough bread in a frying pan with olive oil to make rugged croutons.

THE DRESSING

More often than not, a busy salad needs nothing more than a drizzle of good-quality oil and some salt and pepper. If you need more, see our Flax Oil Salad Dressing (page 185), or the kefir-based dressing on page 75. When making a creamy dressing, think beyond mayonnaise and go for something alive: homemade crème fraîche, kefir or yoghurt.

SMOKED FISH WITH ORANGE & ALMONDS

SERVES 2 AS A MAIN OR 4 WITH OTHER DISHES
PREP TIME: 5 MINS * COOK TIME: 5 MINS
WF | GF | DF | SoF

1 **orange**, halved around its middle

2 tablespoons **flaked almonds**

5–6 **asparagus spears**, thinly sliced into
  ribbons

2–3 generous handfuls of **peppery leaves**,
  watercress is good (about 100g)

2–3 fillets **smoked mackerel** or **trout**
  (about 150g in total), skin removed,
  broken into small chunks

FOR THE DRESSING:

juice of ½ **orange** (from the **orange** above)

½ teaspoon **honey**

1 teaspoon **raw, unpasteurized apple
  cider vinegar** (with mother)

a pinch of **salt**

2 tablespoons **extra virgin olive oil**

Citrus and smoked fish go well from a flavour point of view but they also pack a nutritional punch: the omega-3 from the fish increases gut bacterial diversity while vitamin C is important for supporting our immune system as well as contributing towards growth and repair throughout the body.

Remove the skin and pith from one half of the orange and finely slice into half moons. Juice the other half into a bowl and set aside to use in the dressing.

Toast the almonds in a hot dry pan for a couple of minutes, just until they turn golden, then immediately remove from the pan.

Whisk the rest of the dressing ingredients together with the orange juice and taste for seasoning.

Arrange the asparagus ribbons and the peppery leaves on a serving platter, then top with the orange slices, the smoked fish pieces and the toasted almonds. Drizzle over about half of the dressing to start with, adding more as needed.

Serve immediately.

=TIP=

If asparagus is out of season, use blanched and sliced green beans or broccoli, instead.

SOUR THAI-STYLE SALAD

SERVES 4
PREP TIME: 10 MINS * COOK TIME: 2 MINS
WF | GF

200g **glass/thread noodles**

300g **cucumber**, sliced into ribbons

1 **red chilli**, deseeded or not, finely chopped, or to taste

3 **spring onions**, sliced into small pieces on an angle

150g **green beans**, blanched, drained and cooled

60g **roasted peanuts**, roughly chopped

FOR THE DRESSING:

2 tablespoons **fish sauce**

6cm piece of **lemongrass**, tough outer removed and discarded, very finely chopped

2 teaspoons **raw, unpasteurized apple cider vinegar** (with mother)

juice of 1 **lime**, or more as needed

2 tablespoons **sesame oil**

1 teaspoon **honey**

1 tablespoon **soy sauce/tamari** (choose WF/GF if needed)

Serve this punchy, crunchy salad as a side dish, or use as a base for a rainbow salad (see page 86) with miso-crusted fish like the salmon on page 174, or make it a full meal with some crispy fried tofu, or cooked prawns. Glass noodles (sometimes called thread noodles) are made from mung bean starch.

Boil the kettle. Place the glass noodles into a heatproof bowl and cover with boiling water. Leave for 2 minutes, then drain and rinse in cold water. Set aside. (Or follow the packet instructions – but we find they usually need a bit less time in the hot water.)

Put the cucumber, chilli, spring onions and green beans into a large serving bowl. Toss well.

Stir together the dressing ingredients and taste – it should be salty, tangy and sour. Add a little more lime juice, if needed.

Just before serving, add the cooled noodles and the peanuts to the salad. Pour over half of the dressing and toss again. Taste, adding more dressing as you go – it should be flavourful, but don't make the salad wet. Serve immediately.

=TIP=

Vegetarians and vegans can skip the fish sauce, but may need a touch more salt; vegans can swap the honey for agave.

CELERY, PISTACHIO & BULGUR SALAD

SERVES 2 AS A MAIN OR RAINBOW SALAD BASE (SEE PAGE 86) OR 4 AS A SIDE WITH OTHER DISHES
PREP TIME: 8 MINS * COOK TIME: 15 MINS

DF | V | Ve | SoF

100g **uncooked bulgur wheat**

2 sticks of **celery**

3 tablespoons chopped **shelled, unsalted pistachios**

2 tablespoons finely chopped **flat-leaf parsley**

1 teaspoon finely chopped **chives**

3 tablespoons **pomegranate seeds**

salt, to taste

FOR THE DRESSING:

1 tablespoon **extra virgin olive oil**

½ tablespoon **lemon juice**

a pinch of **salt**

Celery is unfairly confined to being chopped and used in the base of many a stew, soup or sauce, but it's excellent in salads (and a good source of fibre, too).

You can cook the bulgur according to the packet instructions (which usually say to boil it), but we prefer covering it in boiling water, in a lidded pan or covered bowl, with a pinch of salt, and leaving it to soak for about 15 minutes, as this gives it a firmer texture. Whichever you choose, when just tender, drain if necessary and fluff up the grains with a fork. Spread over a plate to cool.

Finely chop the celery. Combine with the pistachios, herbs and pomegranate in a large bowl.

Stir together the dressing ingredients.

Add the cooled bulgur to the bowl and pour in the dressing. Toss well, then taste and add more salt as needed. Serve immediately (the salad keeps in terms of flavour but the herbs will begin to darken over a day, so if you want to make this in advance, add the herbs just before serving).

≡TIP≡

Omit the pomegranate and add some finely chopped apple and some crumbled blue cheese.

EAT THE RAINBOW

LEON-STYLE ROAST VEGETABLES WITH SUMAC-PICKLED ONIONS

SERVES 4

PREP TIME: 10 MINS PLUS 30 MINS DRAINING ★ COOK TIME: 30–40 MINS

WF | GF | DF | V | Ve | NF | SoF

2 **aubergines**, trimmed, halved lengthways

4 tablespoons **extra virgin olive oil**

1 small **cauliflower** and 1 head **broccoli**, stems removed, cut into small florets

1 **red onion**, roughly chopped

1 **celeriac**, peeled, cut into 2cm cubes

6 cloves of **garlic**, peeled

1 sprig of **rosemary**, leaves only

1 sprig of **thyme**, leaves only

salt and **freshly ground black pepper**

FOR THE SUMAC-PICKLED ONIONS:

1 large **red onion**, very finely sliced

100ml **water**

100ml **white wine vinegar**

50ml **raw, unpasteurized apple cider vinegar** (with mother)

1 teaspoon **caster sugar**

1½ teaspoons **salt**

3 teaspoons **sumac**

TO SERVE:

freshly squeezed **lemon juice**

a handful each of **parsley** and **mint leaves**

2 tablespoons **zhoug hot sauce** (see tip), or more to taste

For fans of the LEON paleo box. Good for the gut, even better for your tastebuds.

First, make the pickled onions. Pack the onions into a 500ml lidded jar. In a small saucepan, bring the water, vinegars, sugar and salt to the boil, then remove from the heat and stir in the sumac. Pour into the jar and seal immediately with the lid. The onions can be used as soon as they're cool, but taste best after a few days.

Score the inside flesh of the aubergines with the tip of a knife in a criss-cross pattern. Salt the flesh, making sure to get it into the cuts, and leave to stand on a wire rack, flesh-side down, for 30 minutes.

Meanwhile, heat the oven to 200°C/400°F/gas mark 6.

Gently squeeze out any remaining liquid from the aubergines, then dry with kitchen paper. Cut into wedges and drizzle with 2 tablespoons of the olive oil, season with salt and pepper, and place flesh-side down in a large roasting tray.

Place the cauliflower, broccoli, onion and celeriac in a second large roasting tray. Add the remaining olive oil, garlic cloves, rosemary and thyme leaves, season generously with salt and pepper, and toss to combine. Roast for 30–35 minutes, stirring halfway through, until the vegetables are tender and starting to caramelize. Keep an eye on them, as they may take more or less time. Roast the aubergines at the same time for 25–30 minutes, until lightly charred.

To serve, top the roasted veg with some aubergine, a handful of sumac-pickled onions, a squeeze of lemon, a sprinkling of herbs and a spoonful of zhoug.

=TIP=

Add peanuts or beansprouts or make Ve/V by omitting the prawns and adding crispy fried tofu, instead.

RAINBOW SUMMER ROLLS

SERVES 2–3 AS A MAIN OR 4 WITH OTHER DISHES (MAKES 8)

PREP TIME: 30 MINS

DF | NF

24 cooked and shelled sustainably sourced medium-sized **prawns** (175g)

1 teaspoon **soy sauce/tamari**

150g **cucumber**, deseeded, sliced into thin 4cm strips

1 small **carrot** (50g), sliced into thin 4cm strips

1 **spring onion**, trimmed and sliced into thin 4cm strips

2 **radishes**, cut into matchsticks

a big handful of **coriander leaves**

a big handful of **mint leaves**

8 **rice paper spring roll wrappers**

50g Vietnamese **rice noodles**, covered in boiling water for 3–4 minutes, then drained and rinsed in cold water

FOR THE DIPPING SAUCE:

1½ teaspoons **honey**

1½ tablespoons **fish sauce**

½ **red chilli**, finely chopped

juice of 1 **lime**

Summer rolls are originally from Vietnam and use softened rice paper to enclose bursts of flavour – seafood, fresh herbs, cucumber and onion, among other lovely things – served with a zippy, salty, spicy dipping sauce.

Despite their name, rice noodles sometimes contain wheat, so aren't always GF.

Stir together the dipping sauce ingredients, adding a dash of water if too salty.

Toss the prawns in the soy sauce/tamari and set aside. Prepare the noodles (see ingredients list), all the vegetables and herbs and place within easy reach. Fill a bowl, large enough to dunk the wrappers in, with lukewarm water.

When you're ready to wrap, gently place a rice paper wrapper into the water. Wait until it is just pliable, but not slippery and soft, only 1 minute or so, and remove from the water. Lay it flat on a clean chopping board. Place 3 prawns in a line down the middle of the wrapper. Arrange a little of each vegetable – be mean, not generous – in a line next to the prawns. Top the prawns with a generous amount of coriander and 3–4 mint leaves. Finish with a pinch of the softened noodles, arranged in a neat line next to the prawns. Don't over-fill the delicate wrappers. Fold the top and bottom of each wrapper down over the filling, then fold one side of the wrapper over to cover the filling. Working from the folded side, gently turn the roll over on top of the remaining loose wrapper, quite tightly – this will help close the wrapper but also gently lifts it off the board, without sticking.

Place the roll on a serving plate and repeat until you've finished all 8. Eat immediately, with the dipping sauce alongside.

HOW TO BUILD A RAINBOW SANDWICH

SERVES 1

PREP TIME: 10 MINS

V | NF | SoF

2 slices of good-quality **wholegrain bread** (can be WF/GF)

cream cheese, **soft goats' cheese**, **hummus**, or even **mayo** (can be Ve)

a pinch of finely chopped **chives** (optional)

2 **radishes**, very finely sliced

3–4 very thin slices of raw **beetroot**

a drizzle of **extra virgin olive oil**

3–4 very thin slices of raw **carrot**, cut on an angle

¼ **avocado**, thinly sliced

a small handful of your favourite **salad leaves** (**rocket**, **spinach**, or any **lettuce**)

a handful of **sprouted seeds** (**alfalfa**, **broccoli sprouts**, etc.) (optional)

freshly squeezed lemon juice

salt and **freshly ground black pepper**, to taste

All too often, sandwiches are nothing more than a chunk of cheese stuck between two pieces of bread, eaten on the run and without much thought. Making a rainbow sandwich, packed with raw, colourful vegetables is a slightly whimsical – and silly but fun – way to change that. Our top tips? Include something spreadable, like soft cheese or hummus, to hold it all together, and despite what you might have seen on Instagram, don't make it so full that you can't take a bite! Actual quantities will depend on the size of your bread slices.

Set both slices of bread on a board and top each one generously with your choice of cheese or hummus and a grinding of black pepper.

Next, layer all the ingredients in the order listed on top of one of the slices, adding a little drizzle of oil after the beetroot and finishing with a squeeze of lemon juice, a pinch of salt and some more black pepper. Seasoning with lemon, salt and oil will really draw out the flavour of each vegetable, so don't skip this bit.

Top with the other slice of bread, and eat immediately.

=TIP=

You can swap the cheeses or hummus, and any of the vegetables: they don't all have to be raw, but make sure they go well with other ingredients – for feta cheese, add roasted sweet peppers but omit the sprouts; for thinly sliced mozzarella, go for sliced ripe tomatoes and fresh basil, but take out the carrot.

SMASHED BUTTERNUT & CHEESE ON TOAST

SERVES 2

PREP TIME: 5 MINS * COOK TIME: 45 MINS

V | NF | SoF

1 small **butternut squash**, peeled, deseeded and chopped into 3cm chunks

1 tablespoon **olive oil**

1 teaspoon **extra virgin olive oil**, plus extra for drizzling

4 slices **wholegrain sourdough bread**

80g **feta cheese**, **goats' cheese** or **ricotta**, crumbled

1 **spring onion**, finely chopped, or 1 tablespoon finely chopped **chives**

1 finely chopped **fresh red chilli** or **red chilli flakes** (optional), to serve

salt and **freshly ground black pepper**

Although avo toast is a favourite, we all know we should eat fewer avocados. Even though they're healthy, their cultivation is water intensive and they're often air-freighted. Sweet, silky squash is a great sub (although a completely different dish), especially when paired with cheese. You could also try this with cream cheese spread onto the hot toast. If you don't want cheese, eat with a fried egg instead.

Heat the oven to 180°C/350°F/gas mark 4.

Tumble the squash chunks onto a rimmed baking sheet and drizzle over the olive oil, then toss to combine. Arrange in a single layer on the baking sheet and roast in the oven for about 40 minutes until really tender and soft. It needs to mash easily, so cook for a little longer, if necessary.

Cool the squash slightly, then drizzle over the teaspoon of extra virgin olive oil. Mash roughly, then taste and add a pinch of salt, pepper or extra virgin olive oil, as needed.

Toast the bread and brush with extra virgin olive oil.

Pile and spread the squash onto to the hot toast, pressing down as you go with the prongs of a fork. Scatter over the cheese and then the spring onion or chives and the chilli, if using. Give it a final drizzle of extra virgin olive oil before eating.

═TIP═

There are loads of other on-toast subs for avocado: we love roughly puréed peas or broad beans, whizzed up white beans, with griddled broccoli, or warmed red peppers from a jar with a few anchovies.

EAT THE RAINBOW

KIDNEY BEAN, CORN & CHIPOTLE SOUP

SERVES 4 OR 2 EXTREMELY HUNGRY PEOPLE
PREP TIME: 10 MINS * COOK TIME: 20 MINS
WF | GF | V | NF | SoF

1 tablespoon **extra virgin olive oil**

1 small **onion** finely chopped

1 clove of **garlic**, crushed

¼ teaspoon **ground cumin**

1 teaspoon **smoked paprika** (hot or mild)

1 teaspoon **chipotle paste**

300ml **boiling water**

400g **canned kidney beans**, in water, drained but not rinsed

400g **canned black beans**, in water, drained but not rinsed

100g **courgette**, **yellow courgette** or **summer squash**, chopped into small 1cm cubes

100g **frozen sweetcorn**

TO GARNISH:

100g **feta cheese**, crumbled

1 **spring onion**, finely chopped

freshly squeezed lime juice

A warming, hearty soup, packed with fibre and prebiotics, and so filling you don't even need a wedge of bread on the side.

Heat the oil in a deep, wide pan with a lid over a medium heat. When hot, add the onion and cook for about 10 minutes, stirring often, until soft but not browned. Add the garlic, cumin, paprika and chipotle paste and cook, stirring all the time, for 1 minute, until it all starts to smell delicious and the garlic no longer smells pungent and raw. Add the boiling water and both cans of beans. Bring back to a simmer and cook for 5 minutes. Finally, add the courgette or squash and the sweetcorn and bring back to a simmer again.

Remove from the heat, divide between bowls and top with the crumbled feta, spring onion and a little squeeze of lime juice. Eat immediately.

═TIP═

You can batch-cook and freeze this in advance, but don't add the courgette or sweetcorn. Defrost, reheat and then continue the recipe to serve. In winter, add a handful of kale, rather than summer squash or courgette.

VEGETARIAN RAMEN

SERVES 2

PREP TIME: 10 MINS PLUS 30 MINS SOAKING * COOK TIME: 12–15 MINS

DF | V | NF

FOR THE DASHI STOCK:

20g **dried shiitake mushrooms**

1 sheet of **kombu/dried kelp**

500ml **very hot, not boiling water**

FOR THE BROTH:

1 tablespoon **sesame oil**

2 cloves of **garlic**, crushed

4cm piece of **ginger**, peeled and minced

4 **spring onions**, thinly sliced

1 tablespoon **tomato purée**

1½ tablespoons **red miso paste**

2 tablespoons **sake** (or dry sherry or omit)

1 tablespoon **soy sauce**

1 tablespoon **white sesame seeds**

400ml **unsweetened soy milk**

salt, to taste

TO SERVE:

30g **beansprouts**

1 **pak choi**, stem removed, quartered

2 portions of **ramen noodles**

1 small **carrot**, cut into fine matchsticks

1 **egg**, soft-boiled, halved

2 tablespoons **Kimchi** (page 143), chopped

2 tablespoons **crushed peanuts** (optional)

soy sauce, for drizzling

Satisfying and restorative, this uses vegetarian ingredients to create a rich, tonkotsu-like broth. Fresh ramen noodles are best but dried also work, or they can be swapped for udon or egg noodles. Vegans can leave out the egg. If you can't find kombu, dried bonito flakes will do, but won't be vegetarian.

To make the dashi, soak the mushrooms and kombu in the measured hot water for 30 minutes. Remove the kombu and mushrooms, squeezing their moisture out into the stock. Strain through a sieve and set aside.

To make the broth, heat the sesame oil in a large saucepan over a medium–high heat. Add the garlic, ginger and the white parts of the sliced spring onions and fry until softened and starting to turn golden, 3–4 minutes. Add the tomato purée, red miso, sake, soy sauce and sesame seeds and cook for a further 2–3 minutes until the mixture has darkened. Slowly add all the soy milk, stirring with a wooden spoon to scrape any bits off the bottom of the pan, and mix thoroughly. Finally, add the dashi and stir to combine to a thick, fragrant broth. Taste for seasoning and add salt as required. Reduce the heat to low.

Blanch the beansprouts and pak choi in a large pan of boiling water for 2–3 minutes until tender. Remove with a slotted spoon and set aside.

In the same pan, cook the noodles according to the packet instructions. Drain and divide between 2 bowls.

To serve, ladle the broth over the noodles until they are just about submerged. Top with beansprouts, pak choi, carrots, half an egg, kimchi, spring onion greens, peanuts, if using, and soy sauce. Don't be afraid to slurp.

═TIP═

Red miso is available in large supermarkets, as is cooking sake. Kombu can be ordered online.

BEETROOT & TOMATO RASAM

SERVES 4

PREP TIME: 10 MINS * COOK TIME: 15–20 MINS

WF | GF | V | Ve | NF | SoF

FOR THE RASAM POWDER:
2 **dried red chillies**
2 cloves of **garlic**
1 teaspoon **black peppercorns**
1 teaspoon **coriander seeds**
1 teaspoon **cumin seeds**
½ teaspoon **fenugreek seeds**

FOR THE SOUP:
1 tablespoon **neutral-flavoured cooking oil** (**vegetable**, **sunflower** or **rapeseed**)
2 cloves of **garlic**, crushed
1 teaspoon **mustard seeds**
10–12 **curry leaves**
6 ripe **tomatoes**, roughly chopped
2 **cooked beetroot** (not packed in vinegar), diced into 2cm chunks
2 teaspoons **tamarind paste**
1 teaspoon **salt**, plus more to taste
1 × recipe quantity of **rasam powder** (above)
500ml **water**
2 tablespoons **unsalted butter**
1 large handful of **coriander leaves**, roughly chopped

This is our version of a restorative and fragrant south-Indian soup. Store-bought rasam powders are available, if you are in a hurry, but making your own will elevate this dish. It also means you can tweak it to your taste.

To make the rasam powder, toast all the ingredients in a hot, dry frying pan until fragrant, 1–2 minutes. Allow to cool, then grind to a coarse powder with a pestle and mortar (or a spice grinder).

To make the soup, heat the oil in a large saucepan over a medium–high heat. Add the garlic, mustard seeds and curry leaves, and fry for 1–2 minutes until fragrant and the mustard seeds start to pop. Add the tomatoes and fry for 4–5 minutes until they start to soften, then add the beetroot chunks and fry for a further 3 minutes. Next, add the tamarind paste, breaking it up and mixing it in with a wooden spoon. Cook for a further minute or so. Add the salt, rasam powder and measured water, mix well, then bring to the boil. Cook for 5 minutes.

If you like the soup more broth-like, leave as it is. We like it a bit thicker, so use a stick blender to give the mixture a very quick blitz, leaving it chunky.

Taste for seasoning and add salt, if necessary.

Stir through the butter until melted, then add the coriander leaves. Divide between bowls and eat immediately.

EAT THE RAINBOW

=TIP=

Rasam is
sometimes made
with added
cooked lentils.

≡TIP≡

Make this NF by leaving out the almonds.

ROAST ROOTS & GREEN GOAT DRESSING

SERVES 4 WITH OTHER DISHES OR 2 AS A MAIN COURSE
PREP TIME: 10 MINS * COOK TIME: 45 MINS
WF | GF | V

FOR THE DRESSING:

3–4 tablespoons soft and creamy rindless **goats' cheese**

1 tablespoon roughly chopped **chives**

1 tablespoon roughly chopped **dill**

1 tablespoon roughly chopped **flat-leaf parsley**

a small handful of roughly chopped **watercress**

1 teaspoon **raw, unpasteurised apple cider vinegar** (with mother)

1 teaspoon **white miso**

1 tablespoon **full-fat plain live yoghurt**

1 small clove of **garlic** (optional)

a pinch of **salt**, or as needed

FOR THE VEGETABLES:

2 **carrots**, sliced on an angle into 2cm pieces

400g **beetroot** (any kind), trimmed and quartered

a drizzle of **olive oil**

salt and **freshly ground black pepper**

TO SERVE:

a knob of **butter** (optional)

2 tablespoons **flaked almonds** (optional)

This dressing is our spin on green goddess dressing, a slightly retro recipe (which we love). Instead of the more usual mayo and sour cream, we use goats' cheese, yoghurt and a tiny bit of miso, for a wonderfully savoury, umami-laden herby green dressing. It's so good that we often make double quantities and keep leftovers for salads and sandwich fillings.

Heat the oven to 180°C/350°F/gas mark 4.

Place the carrots on a piece of kitchen foil large enough to enclose them. Season with salt and pepper, then add a drizzle of olive oil and toss so they're well covered. Wrap in the foil.

Repeat for the beetroot.

Place the foil parcels on a baking sheet and roast in the oven for 45 minutes. Remove and unwrap, then arrange the vegetables on a serving plate.

Meanwhile, place all the dressing ingredients into a small jug blender, or use a stick blender, and whizz until bright green and really smooth. Taste and add more salt, as needed.

To toast the almonds, heat the butter in a pan over a low heat and add the almonds. Cook until lightly browned, about 1–2 minutes, then remove from the heat.

Serve warm or at room temperature. Drizzle a few spoonfuls of the dressing over the vegetables and sprinkle with the toasted almonds just before you serve.

HOW TO MAKE AN AWESOME SLAW

SERVES 4–6
PREP TIME: 12 MINS
WF | GF | DF | V | NF | SoF

FOR THE SLAW:
¼ **red cabbage**, thinly sliced
¼ **white cabbage**, thinly sliced
6 **spring onions**, white and light green
    parts only, thinly sliced
1 **carrot**, grated
1 **apple**, cored and grated
a small bunch of **coriander leaves**,
    roughly chopped
50g **sunflower seeds**

FOR THE DRESSING:
3 tablespoons **extra virgin olive oil**
2 tablespoons **raw, unpasteurized apple**
    cider vinegar (with mother)
2 teaspoons **Dijon mustard**
2 teaspoons **honey**
salt and **freshly ground black pepper,**
    to taste

≡TIP≡

To get the vegetables
as thin as possible, try
using a mandoline or a
spiralizer.

We've all had a bad experience with greasy, room-temperature, over-mayo-ed coleslaw, but things don't have to be that way. Slaws are a great way to get raw veg into your diet. What's more, they go well with a wide range of dishes. This is a recipe for a basic slaw, but the possibilities really are endless. Throw in some nuts for a dose of polyphenols. Add roasted pumpkin seeds for crunch. Play around with different types of acid – citrus juice is not only delicious but the vitamin C helps liberate the other nutrients. Try using different oils for their respective health benefits, such as walnut oil, avocado oil, rapeseed oil and sesame oil. If you miss the mayo creaminess of traditional coleslaw, try using plain live yoghurt of any kind (or Milk Kefir, see page 155) instead. The basic principles are shredded raw veg with an acidic dressing to lightly 'cook' the vegetables and help make them easier to digest (not to mention tastier).

To match this with Mexican-style food, add a spoonful of crème fraîche, a pinch of chilli, lime juice and some chipotle paste to the dressing. For Thai dishes add Thai basil, finely chopped lemongrass and red chilli. For Japanese-style meals, skip the mustard in the dressing and the apple in the salad, add some sesame seeds and make the dressing with soy sauce, sesame oil and a little spoonful of mayo... you get the idea: slaw is highly adaptable.

Place all the slaw ingredients in a large mixing bowl and toss to combine.

To make the dressing, whisk together all the ingredients in a small bowl until fully emulsified, adding salt and pepper to taste.

Pour the dressing over the vegetables and mix thoroughly until glossy and fully coated in the dressing.

ROAST BROCCOLI & BEANS WITH TAHINI SAUCE

SERVES 4 AS A SIDE OR 2 AS A MAIN
PREP TIME: 4 MINS * COOK TIME: 7–8 MINS
WF | GF | DF | V | Ve | NF | SoF

150g **green beans**
200g **broccoli**, ideally tenderstem or
  purple sprouting
2 tablespoons **olive oil**
a pinch of **salt**
about 1 tablespoon **pomegranate
  molasses**

FOR THE TAHINI SAUCE:
2 tablespoons **tahini** (look for a brand with
  minimal bitterness)
2 teaspoons **lemon juice**, or to taste
1 clove of **garlic**, crushed to a paste
a pinch of **salt**, or to taste
water, as needed

≡TIP≡

If you want to make these
vegetables for a Japanese-style
meal, omit the lemon juice and
add 1½ heaped teaspoons miso
paste, ½ teaspoon sesame oil,
1 teaspoon soy sauce, ½ teaspoon
mirin or a pinch of sugar and
1 teaspoon or so of lime juice, then
thin with water.

Some of you might have childhood memories of mushy broccoli and limp boiled beans, but this couldn't be further from that. The green vegetables are quickly roasted, giving the broccoli a delicious char but staying crisp, before being doused in a nutty, lemony tahini sauce and a drizzle of pomegranate molasses.

Heat the oven to 200°C/400°F/gas mark 6.

Tumble the beans and broccoli onto a large rimmed baking sheet, then add the oil and a pinch of salt. Toss, working the oil into the broccoli florets, then arrange in a single layer. Roast in the oven for 7–8 minutes, or until the broccoli heads are just beginning to char (don't let them burn, though).

Make the tahini sauce: mix together the tahini, lemon juice, garlic and salt. You will notice that, as you stir, the tahini thickens and darkens – this is fine, but you will need to add enough water to thin it to a pourable consistency. Do so, adding 1 tablespoon or so at a time. Taste, and add more salt or lemon, if needed.

When the vegetables are ready, transfer them to a warmed platter. Spread out, then drizzle with the tahini sauce and finally, sparingly, with the pomegranate molasses. Serve immediately.

EAT THE RAINBOW

SPINACH WITH RAISINS & PINE NUTS

SERVES 4 AS A SIDE OR 2 ON TOAST
PREP TIME: 5 MINS * COOK TIME: 10 MINS
WF | GF | DF | V | Ve | SoF

250g **spinach**, washed and still wet
1 tablespoon **olive oil**
25g **pine nuts**
25g **raisins**
1 clove of **garlic**, very finely chopped
a knob of **butter** (optional, omit if DF/Ve)
a pinch of **salt**
a drizzle of **extra virgin olive oil** (optional)
a squeeze of **lemon juice** (optional)

This is one of those curious dishes that is much, much more than the sum of its parts – the pine nuts give a toasty flavour and subtle crunch, the raisins plump up in the buttery oil and the whole thing is irresistible.

Set a large lidded pan over a medium heat and add 2 tablespoons of water. Add the wet spinach, cover with the lid and cook for 1–2 minutes until just wilted but not completely cooked. Drain in a colander, using the back of a spoon to press out some of the excess liquid.

Set a large frying pan over a medium heat and add the olive oil. When hot, add the pine nuts and raisins and cook just until the pine nuts begin to turn golden, then add the garlic and cook for 1 minute longer. Next, add the butter and the spinach. Cook, stirring, until the spinach has completely wilted. If it releases a lot more liquid, you may want to cook it a little longer to let it bubble off – but don't pour it away as you will lose a lot of flavour.

Season with salt and finish with a drizzle of extra virgin olive oil, if you like. A squeeze of lemon brightens the flavours, too. Eat hot or warm.

=TIP=

This is excellent alongside fish dishes.

POMEGRANATE & PISTACHIO QUINOA

SERVES 4 AS A SIDE OR USE AS A RAINBOW SALAD BASE

PREP TIME: 15 MINS * COOK TIME: 20 MINS

WF | GF | DF | V | Ve | SoF

100g **uncooked quinoa**

100g **cucumber**, finely chopped

40g **shelled, roasted pistachios** (**salted** or **unsalted**), roughly chopped

3 tablespoons chopped **dill**

3 tablespoons chopped **flat-leaf parsley**

2 tablespoons finely chopped **chives** or **spring onion**

75g **pomegranate seeds**

2 tablespoons **extra virgin olive oil**

2 teaspoons **lemon juice**, or more to taste

salt, to taste

Rebecca makes salads like this A LOT, to serve with everything from griddled halloumi to summertime roast chicken.

Rinse the quinoa well under cold running water. Cook according to the packet instructions, or measure the quinoa's volume and use 2 parts water to 1 part quinoa and simmer in a covered pan for 15–20 minutes. Once cooked, drain off any remaining water and spread the quinoa over a plate to cool.

Once cooled, tip into a salad bowl and add the cucumber, nuts, herbs and pomegranate seeds. Stir together the extra virgin olive oil and lemon juice and use it to dress the salad. Taste and add salt, if needed (it will be unless you cooked the quinoa in stock). Eat immediately.

≡TIP≡

See the page on rainbow salads (page 86) for more on how to use this as a rainbow salad base.

SWEET POTATO PATATAS BRAVAS

SERVES 4 WITH OTHER DISHES

PREP TIME: 12 MINS ✷ COOK TIME: 30 MINS

WF | GF | DF | V | Ve | NF | SoF

600g **sweet potatoes**, skin-on, cut into
2cm cubes
2 tablespoons **olive oil**
½ teaspoon **smoked paprika**
salt and **freshly ground black pepper**

FOR THE SAUCE:
1 tablespoon **olive oil**
1 **onion**, very finely chopped
1 clove of **garlic**, very finely chopped
up to 1 tablespoon very finely chopped
red chilli, to taste
1 teaspoon **hot** or **mild smoked paprika**
300g **passata**
1 teaspoon **raw, unpasteurized apple
cider vinegar** (with mother)
salt and **freshly ground black pepper**

FOR THE FAUX ALIOLI:
3 tablespoons good-quality **mayo**
(can be Ve)
2 teaspoons **extra virgin olive oil**
1½ teaspoons **lemon juice**
1 small clove of **garlic**, crushed to a paste
with the flat of a knife blade

Traditionally, patatas bravas are made with white potatoes, but sweet potatoes come with more fibre and fewer starches. Their slight sweetness contrasts neatly with the tart, subtly spicy sauce.

Heat the oven to 200°C/400°F/gas mark 6.

Combine the potatoes, oil, smoked paprika and seasoning in a very large roasting tray and toss to combine. Spread out in an even layer and roast in the hot oven for 30 minutes, tossing again halfway through cooking, until the potatoes are tender and the cut edges have begun to char and crisp up.

Meanwhile, make the sauce. Heat the oil in a saucepan over a medium heat. When hot, add the onion and a pinch of salt. Cook, stirring, for up to 10 minutes, or until the onion is translucent but not browned. Add the garlic and red chilli and cook for 1 minute, then add the smoked paprika and the passata. Stir well and bring up to a simmer. Cook for 10 minutes or so, or until the mixture is saucy. If it gets too thick, add a splash of water. Finally add the cider vinegar. Taste and add salt and pepper, as needed, or more smoked paprika or vinegar, if you like. The sauce should be tangy, with a hint of smoke and some warm spicy heat.

Stir the faux alioli ingredients together.

Tip the cooked potatoes into a serving bowl, spoon over some of the sauce and drizzle over a little of the alioli, or serve on the side, if you prefer. Eat hot.

BROCCOLI WITH CRUMBS, CHILLI & ANCHOVY

SERVES 4 AS A SIDE

PREP TIME: 3 MINS * COOK TIME: 12 MINS

DF | NF | SoF

2 tablespoons **olive oil**, or more as needed

3 **anchovies in oil**

2 large slices of **day-old wholegrain sourdough bread**, shredded into rough 1cm pieces

1–3 teaspoons finely chopped **red chilli**, deseeded, or to taste

1 clove of **garlic**, crushed (optional)

a generous pinch of **fennel seeds** (optional)

250g **purple** or **tenderstem broccoli**, sliced into 3–4cm lengths

Serve as a side or as a warm salad, or toss through freshly cooked pasta (or Gram Flour Pasta, page 37).

Heat the olive oil in your widest frying pan over a medium heat. Add the anchovies and let them melt in the pan, stirring a few times so they don't catch and burn. Add the shredded bread and cook, turning often, until golden and crisp. If the bread is browning too fast, reduce the heat. Add a splash more oil if the pan seems very dry. When the bread is almost done, add the chilli, garlic and fennel seeds, if using, and cook for 2 minutes, just until the garlic is fragrant and no longer smells raw.

Blanch the broccoli in a pan of boiling salted water for 2 minutes (we like it really crisp – cook it longer if you don't). Drain and let it steam briefly in the colander, as any water left on the broccoli will make the crumbs soggy.

Toss the broccoli and crumbs together, scraping up every last bit of the now deliciously flavoured oil. Serve hot or warm.

=TIP=

Tear over some buffalo mozzarella or even serve arranged around a plump, creamy burrata, with a drizzle of extra extra virgin olive oil.

EAT THE RAINBOW

CUCUMBER, SEAWEED & SESAME SALAD

SERVES 4 AS A SIDE
PREP TIME: 15 MINS
WF | GF | DF | V | Ve | NF

2 tablespoons **dried wakame seaweed**

300g **cucumber**, cut into thin rounds

a pinch of **salt**

½ **avocado**, cubed into 1cm pieces
(optional)

a pinch of **toasted white sesame seeds**

FOR THE DRESSING

2 tablespoons **rice wine vinegar**

a pinch of **salt**

a generous pinch of **sugar**

1 teaspoon **soy sauce/tamari** (choose
GF if needed)

A great way to add prebiotic fibre to Japanese-style meals. Serve alongside soy-glazed fish or chicken, or with Crispy Fried Almost-Raw Vegetables (see page 47) or Crispy Sweet Potato Fritters (see page 51) and some brown rice.

Put the seaweed in a bowl, cover with boiling water and set aside. Place the cucumber and salt in a bowl and set aside, too.

After about 10 minutes, drain the seaweed and, once cool enough to handle, roughly chop. Pour away any liquid that has been drawn out of the cucumber.

Stir together the dressing ingredients.

Place the cucumber and seaweed in a serving bowl, pour over half of the dressing and toss. Add the avocado pieces, if using, and the sesame seeds and drizzle over the rest of the dressing. Serve immediately.

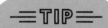

≡TIP≡

Wakame seaweed is available online and in Japanese food shops. It comes dried and a packet lasts almost forever, so it's a good investment.

EAT
LIVELY

Foods with plentiful live, active cultures help to promote the good bacteria in our guts, keeping them happy and healthy.

MISO BUTTER

This is deliciously like Marmite if you spread it straight onto toast. It's salty, too, so spread as thinly as you would Marmite. We use this umami flavour bomb on sautéed mushrooms, but it's also extremely good melted onto roasted sweet potatoes, smeared on top of just-cooked burgers, steak or grilled chicken, brushed over seared salmon, broccoli, aubergine... As a general rule, look for an unpasteurized, live brand, and try to add it once food is off the heat, as cooking miso kills the beneficial bacteria in it.

For each recipe, stir together until combined. Store in a sealed jar or tub, in the fridge, until needed.

PLAIN MISO BUTTER

PREP TIME: 2 MINS

WF | GF | V | NF

2 tablespoons **butter** (salted if using for cooking; unsalted if spreading)

2 tablespoons **miso paste**

SALTY MISO SPREAD

PREP TIME: 2 MINS

WF | GF | V | NF

2 tablespoons **unsalted butter**
2 tablespoons **miso paste**
2 tablespoons **tahini**

Tahini turns this into a fantastically nutty spread, or something to melt over roasted vegetables. As above, don't be too liberal with this — it's still salty.

SWEET & SALTY MISO SPREAD

PREP TIME: 2 MINS

WF | GF | V | NF

2 tablespoons **unsalted butter**

2 tablespoons **miso paste**

2 tablespoons **tahini**

2 tablespoons **unrefined dark brown sugar** (or use good-quality honey)

Melt onto hot toast.

STEVE'S SOURDOUGH BREAD

MAKES 2 LOAVES

PREP TIME: 1 HOUR PLUS UP TO 31 HOURS PROVING AND RESTING * COOK TIME: 1 HOUR 40 MINS

DF | V | Ve | NF | SoF

FOR THE STARTER:

100g **strong white bread flour** (or a mixture of **bread flour** and **rye flour**), plus 2 tablespoons each time you feed it

100ml **water**, plus 2 tablespoons each time you feed it

FOR THE LEVAIN:

100ml **starter** (see above)

100g **strong white bread flour**

100g **tepid water**

FOR THE BREAD:

240g **levain** (see above)

800g **strong white bread flour**, plus more for dusting

200g **wholemeal bread flour**

660ml **slightly warmer than lukewarm water**

1½ teaspoons **fine salt**

polenta, for dusting

Steve, Rebecca's husband and the LEON Happy photographer, started making sourdough in lockdown. He has kept doing it, as it saves the family at least £300 a year, compared to buying it. Also, he just really likes the process.

A lot of sourdough recipes make it sound like the timings have to be religiously adhered to, but that's not the case. Steve fits bread-making into his normal life. Sourdough is pretty robust, and he often stalls the process by putting half-finished dough in the fridge for a day, until he has time to attend to it or until he's ready to bake it. He makes two loaves at a time, as it's no more difficult and you can freeze the spare.

Get the best-quality bread flour you can find. The price variation isn't huge, and it really makes a difference. You will also need: two mixing bowls, two proving baskets or bannetons (not essential but very useful), a dough scraper and an oven-proof cast-iron casserole dish with a lid (this will blacken with use!).

To make the starter, mix the flour and water in a bowl. Cover with a clean tea towel and leave in a warm place for 48 hours. If small bubbles appear on the surface, wild yeasts have colonised the dough and you have a starter. Remove and discard half of the starter (or store it in a pot in the fridge, ready to be used in brownies, see page 152, or pancakes).

Feed the starter, almost every day, with 2 tablespoons of strong white bread flour and 2 tablespoons of water. Each time, remove about a quarter to a half, and either keep or discard in your food waste bin (unless you bake bread so often that you need almost all of it – if you miss a day or two, it will survive).

A day before you want to bake bread, start making a levain. First, remove 100ml of the starter from the fridge and allow it to warm over 4–5 hours. Stir in 100g strong white bread flour and 100g of tepid water. Place in a large jar and put an elastic band around its middle, marking where the mixture comes to. Leave somewhere warm for 4–6 hours, or overnight in cooler weather, until doubled in size.

When ready to make your bread, divide the levain in half (about 120g each) and put each half into a bowl. Add half of each of the flours to each bowl, then add half of the lukewarm water to each bowl. Mix together, using your hands. Cover each bowl with a damp tea towel and leave for 1 hour.

Add half the fine salt to each dough along with a splash of water, mixing it together thoroughly with your hands. Re-cover and let rest somewhere warm for half an hour (a closed oven with the light on is a good place – touch the dough to check – if it feels hot, that's too warm).

Wet your hands and fold the dough in on itself in the bowl, from the top, bottom and both sides, then scoop up each dough and turn over. Re-cover and return to the warm place to continue proving. Repeat this 3 more times, at 30-minute intervals. Then leave the doughs, covered again, for 2 hours.

To pre-shape the dough, loosen each from the bowl with your hands and tip onto a clean work surface. Don't use any flour – you want it to stick. Use a dough scraper or spatula to turn the dough, using quick flicking motions under the dough, to rotate and twist it while letting it stick to the counter – this builds up tension, nudging the dough into a tight ball and retaining all the air pockets. Cover with a damp cloth and leave for 30 minutes.

Turn the dough balls upside down and dust the upturned side and your hands with flour. Pull the dough towards you then fold it up onto itself. Do the same a couple of times on each side, and finally stretch out the top side slightly and pull it down, then do this again and once more, to form a ball again. Use the scraper to pre-shape the dough again, as above, building up the tension.

=TIP=

Soak and wash up as you go. Nothing will put you off making bread as quickly as a heap of bowls with 2-day-old dough crusted onto them. Use your hands to remove most of the dough, not a brush or scourer, which will gum up immediately.

Liberally dust 2 proving baskets (bannetons) with flour, massaging it into the cracks. Flip each dough over and place in the baskets. Cover with a damp cloth and place in the fridge for 10–24 hours. (After 10 hours have passed, the time just depends on when you have room in your day to bake the loaves.)

When ready to cook, heat the oven to 240°C/475°F/gas mark 9. Place a cast-iron casserole dish with a lid into the oven, with the lid resting on top but not fitted in place (or it will expand and stick), to heat up for 10 minutes.

Dust the top side of one loaf, still in the proving basket, with polenta. Gently loosen the dough from the sides of the basket. Remove the hot dish carefully from the oven and tip the dough directly into it, so that the polenta-dusted area becomes the bottom. Don't worry if it falls in slightly wonkily, just quickly and gently move the dough so that it's in the middle of the dish. Using a serrated knife, slash each side of the loaf's top with a curved line, almost from top to bottom. Place the lid on the dish and bake the bread in the oven for 40 minutes. Then remove the lid and bake for a final 8 minutes. Remove from the oven and use 2 wooden spoons to lift the bread out.

Repeat to cook the other loaf.

Try to resist tearing into the bread when it's really hot as all its precious moisture will rush out as steam. Cool the second loaf and store in the freezer, well-sealed in a bag or an air-tight container.

MISO SOUP

SERVES 4
PREP TIME: 2 MINS * COOK TIME: 5-10 MINS
WF | GF | DF | V | Ve | NF

2 tablespoons **dried wakame seaweed**

1 litre hot **chicken** or **vegetable stock**, or **dashi**

2–3 tablespoons **miso paste**, depending on flavour and saltiness, to taste

2 **spring onions**, finely chopped

200g **silken tofu**, drained and gently cubed into 1cm pieces

Miso soup is so easy to make and is a very gut-friendly dish, because of the rich miso paste and prebiotic seaweed. If you don't do soya, leave out the tofu and look for a soy-free miso, often made with barley.

Cover the seaweed in boiling water and set aside.

Bring the stock to a simmer in a pan, then stir in the miso, whisking until smooth. Drain the soaked seaweed, discarding the liquid, and add to the pan. Just before serving, add the spring onions.

Divide the tofu between 4 warmed soup bowls, then ladle the broth on top. Serve immediately.

≡TIP≡
We sometimes have a late-morning mug of miso and seaweed instead of a cup of tea.

IDEAS FOR CHEESE

As with much of nutrition science, our understanding of why cheese might be good for the gut is in the early stages. However, from a few small studies, it looks as though eating full-fat, unprocessed cheeses, that have had some time to ferment and develop a colony of their own good bacteria, may have a positive effect on gut health and the population of our microbiome.

The best cheeses for this seem to be those made with raw milk (although some made with pasteurized milk, such as feta, also contain live microbes). Many cheeses with a 'protected designation of origin', or PDO, label have to be made with raw milk to qualify for that status. This is true for lots of French cheeses, including Brie, Camembert and Roquefort, as well as Italian cheeses like Parmiagiano reggiano and Gorgonzola. In fact, many artisanal cheesemakers reckon their products taste better with unpasteurized milk and choose to use it.

Staff in a good cheese shop should be able to tell you which ones are unpasteurized, and supermarket cheeses state this on the packaging. (Pregnant women are advised not to eat unpasteurized cheeses that are soft and haven't been aged.) On the other hand, soft cheeses that are made to be eaten while very fresh, like mozzarella or cottage cheeses, don't have time to ferment much, so won't contain much bacteria.

There are also plenty of fermented vegan cheeses on the market, often made with live cultures as part of their fermentation process.

Cooking any cheese will kill its bacteria, so when you're adding cheese to a hot meal, add it at the end, off the heat. We love melted cheesy deliciousness as much as the next person, so this is not a ban on cooked cheese. But ideally, eat cheese at room temperature to get its goodness.

TRUE BLUE

Crumble blue cheese into salads or over grilled vegetables.

BOOST YOUR BURGER

Dot the top of a steak or burger with a crumble of blue cheese after cooking.

MOREISH SIDES

Top hot, creamy polenta with a handful of Parmesan or pecorino.

MEXICAN FLAVOURS

Use feta to top baked sweet potatoes, bean soups or chilli and even beans on toast.

A TASTE OF THE EAST

Try feta or labneh in wraps with falafel, cucumber and lettuce.

SWEET SALADS

Toss feta into a salad of peas and asparagus, or use a crumbly rinded goats' cheese.

SWITCH UP YOUR SARNIES

Swap cheese and pickle for Comté and chutney; or Brie, tomato and basil; or Morbier with fried onions; or blue cheese with pear and chopped walnuts.

LIVELY PASTA

Toss a handful of blue cheese into just-cooked pasta, with a handful of fried sage leaves and some toasted hazelnuts.

OUT OF THE ROASTING TIN

Dot labneh or crumbled goats' cheese over roasted vegetables.

PUDDINGS

Make a traditional (unbaked) cheesecake using live cream cheese, or even kefir cream cheese.

HOMEMADE PIZZA

When making your own pizza, try adding cheese just as it comes out of the oven: crumbed goats' cheese or blue cheese go brilliantly with broccoli, roasted on the pizza itself, or add a shaving of sharp and salty pecorino along with a handful of rocket and some good-quality parma ham.

A CHEESY FINALE

Skip pudding and have a cheese board instead. Is there a more gut-friendly meal than lively cheese, wholegrain crackers or rye crackers (see page 71), served with raw crudités like celery, or sliced apple and a handful of grapes? Add in some homemade proper pickles and a few slices of sourdough bread and you're winning!

CHICORY, RADISH & BLUE CHEESE SALAD

SERVES 4 AS A SIDE
PREP TIME: 10 MINS
WF | GF | V | NF | SoF

1 head **chicory**, trimmed and separated into individual leaves, large leaves sliced in half
4 **radishes**, finely sliced
1 teaspoon finely chopped **dill**
1 teaspoon finely chopped **parsley**
Flax Oil Salad Dressing (see page 185), but swap the **Dijon mustard** for **wholegrain mustard**
100g **blue cheese**, crumbled

This little salad may have only a handful of ingredients, but it's a nutritional powerhouse: the flax oil dressing delivers some omega-3, the cheese contains live cultures and protein, and the vegetables provide some of our daily, much needed, fibre. Adding a handful of unpasteurized cheese to a salad like this is an excellent way to introduce a few more good microbes into your diet. Quick to make, delicious to eat.

Place the chicory leaves and radishes into a mixing bowl.

Make the dressing, remembering to omit the Dijon mustard and use wholegrain instead. Add the finely chopped herbs to the dressing and stir well. Pour half the dressing over the leaves and toss, gently.

Arrange the leaves on a serving platter, and scatter over the blue cheese. Finish with a little more of the dressing, as needed. Eat straight away, or the chicory will start to discolour.

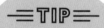

≡TIP≡

No chicory? Use little gem instead. No blue cheese? Try Parmesan, goats' cheese or a crumbly sharp cheese.

CHARRED COURGETTES WITH LABNEH & ZA'ATAR

SERVES 4 WITH OTHER DISHES OR 2 AS A MAIN COURSE
PREP TIME: 2 MINS * COOK TIME: 5 MINS
WF | GF | V | NF | SoF

2 **courgettes**, cut on an angle into 1.5cm-
thick slices
extra virgin olive oil, for cooking
200g **Labneh** (see page 149) (you can also
use ready-made **kefir cheese**, or **feta**)
extra virgin olive oil, for drizzling
1–2 teaspoons **za'atar**, to taste
flaky sea salt, to taste

Za'atar is a spice blend containing sesame seeds, thyme and sour sumac. If you don't have it, mild chilli flakes, black pepper and a pinch of sesame seeds work very well, too.

Place a griddle pan or large frying pan over a high heat. When the pan is really hot, add a splash of olive oil. When the oil is hot, add the courgettes, arranging in a single layer. Cook for 1–2 minutes, or until they begin to char, then use tongs to turn each piece. The aim is to get some nice dark-brown caramelization, but without the courgettes cooking through and collapsing. As soon as they are charred all over, remove from the pan and arrange on a serving plate.

Taste the labneh – you might want to add a pinch of salt, in which case stir it in well. Dot the labneh over the courgettes, then drizzle with extra virgin olive oil. Scatter over the za'atar and a little flaky salt, then serve.

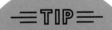
≡TIP≡

If you prefer to serve this at room temperature, let the courgettes cool before adding the other ingredients.

MISO GARLIC MUSHROOMS

SERVES 4 AS A SIDE
PREP TIME: 5 MINS ✷ COOK TIME: 10 MINS
WF | GF | V | NF

1 tablespoon **extra virgin olive oil**,
for cooking
200g **mushrooms**, sliced 5mm thick
or quartered
1 clove of **garlic**, crushed to a paste
1 tablespoon **unsalted butter**
1–2 teaspoons **miso paste**
a pinch of **toasted black sesame seeds**
(optional)

Although fermented miso paste is a Japanese ingredient, these incredibly savoury mushrooms go with dishes from all over the world. As well as with Japanese food, we like them on toast, as a side to chicken, on top of creamy polenta (see page 52), with risotto, or even as a sauce for gnocchi.

Heat the oil in a wide sauté pan over a medium heat. When hot, add the mushrooms and cook, stirring often, until they begin to turn a golden caramel colour. They are ready when they are coloured all over, but not collapsing. Add the garlic and cook for 1 minute.

Meanwhile, mix the butter and 1 teaspoon of the miso paste together, adding the second spoonful of miso, if needed, once you've tasted it.

Remove from the heat and add the miso butter to the pan. Stir to melt and coat the mushrooms with the mixture, then add the sesame seeds, if using. Serve immediately.

=≡TIP≡=

We like chestnut
mushrooms for this, but
you can use any firm
mushroom.

KIMCHI

MAKES A 1-LITRE JAR

PREP TIME: 12 MINS * COOK TIME: 15 MINS PLUS UP TO 2 WEEKS FERMENTING

WF | GF | DF | V | Ve | NF

1 head **Chinese leaf cabbage**, core removed, leaves roughly chopped, washed in a solution of 1 litre **cold water** + 35g **coarse (non-iodized) rock** or **sea salt**, then drained well

40g **coarse (non-iodized) rock** or **sea salt**

4cm piece of **fresh ginger**, peeled

6 cloves of **garlic**, peeled

2½ tablespoons **fish sauce** (if Ve, can use **vegan 'fish' sauce**, a spoonful of **miso paste** or just **soy sauce**)

1 tablespoon **soy sauce/tamari** (choose GF if needed)

1 teaspoon **hot chilli flakes**

3 teaspoons **mild chilli powder** (or more if using **Korean gochugaru** – it's fairly mild but gives traditional kimchi its red colour)

1 **mooli/daikon/Asian radish** (about 225g), peeled and cut into thin matchsticks

3 **spring onions**, well washed of any soil, trimmed and cut on an angle into 1cm pieces

1-litre sterilized **glass jar with a lid**

While there are loads of recipes out there for quick kimchi, the proper, probiotic-filled stuff needs plenty of time to develop. If you don't want to wait, buy an unpasteurized kimchi from your local Asian store, but keep an eye on the sodium content which can be very high in shop-bought versions.

Thoroughly massage the salt into the drained cabbage. Place in a bowl and leave in the fridge overnight, turning once or twice.

The next day, blitz the ginger, garlic, fish sauce (if using) and soy sauce, chilli flakes and powder into a paste in a small food processor. Add a dash of water if necessary.

Drain the salted cabbage and rinse it well, then wash it in 2 changes of clean water, massaging it again to remove any remaining lumps of salt. Drain.

Place the cabbage back into a large bowl with the radish and spring onions, then pour the spice paste on top. Use a spoon or gloved hands to work the mixture into the vegetables until well coated, then spoon into the sterilized jar. Press down with the back of the spoon to leave a 3–5cm headspace. Seal and leave at a steady room temperature (ideally 18–22°C) out of direct sunlight. It will start to ferment in less than 1 day in high summer, or up to 5 days if your home is cool. Release the lid at least daily to allow any fermenting gases to escape, press the kimchi back down into the brine with a clean spoon, then re-seal. (You could use a pickle weight for this.)

To check fermentation, look for bubbles in the brine when you tap the jar. Once it has got going, place in the fridge for at least 1 week, preferably 2. It will keep for up to 2 months in the fridge. Always use clean spoons and make sure to press down the vegetables so that they are always covered with the brine.

SAUERKRAUT

MAKES A 1-LITRE JAR

PREP TIME: 2 MINS ★ COOK TIME: 10–15 MINS PLUS 1 WEEK FERMENTING

WF | GF | DF | V | Ve | NF | SoF

1kg **white cabbage**, shredded
1 tablespoon **coarse sea salt**

1-litre sterilized **glass jar with a lid**

Proper fermented cabbage is a thing of probiotic joy, and we have been known to use it in burgers (instead of melted cheese), with cream cheese or smoked fish (or both) in a rye-bread sandwich, or on the side of rich or smoky meat dishes.

Place the cabbage in a large bowl, then sprinkle over the salt. Toss, then set aside for 5 minutes. The cabbage will start to release its juices, but will need some help. If you know anyone who makes sauerkraut regularly, borrow their cabbage crusher; if not, get to work with a potato masher or knead it with your hands and fists, pressing the cabbage to help it release water. This process creates the pickling liquor, so keep going for 5–10 minutes. When ready, the cabbage will be soft and there will plenty of liquid in the bowl.

Tightly pack the cabbage into the sterilized jar, pushing the cabbage down into the pickling liquor with the back of a clean spoon to leave a 3–5cm headspace. Anything exposed to the air may go mouldy so use a pickle weight if you have one. Seal the lid, loosely if possible, and leave at a steady room temperature out of direct sunlight. Every day, release the lid to allow any fermenting gases to escape, then re-seal, pushing the pickle under the brine again, if necessary. Always use clean spoons and make sure to press down the cabbage so that it is always covered with the brine. Start tasting after 1 week. Once you feel it is ready, store in the fridge. It will keep for up to 2 months in the fridge.

=TIP=

This makes quite a lot so, although it keeps, it is fun to transfer some to a smaller jar, as a gift.

PERFECT PICKLE

MAKES ABOUT 800ML

PREP TIME: 10 MINS * COOK TIME: 10 MINS PLUS FERMENTING TIME

NF | SoF

175g **cauliflower** (about ½ head), cut into small pieces (save any leaves and add a few, well washed and finely sliced, to the pickle jar, too)

400g **carrots**, peeled and coarsely grated

10g **sea** or **rock salt** (about 1 scant tablespoon, but since crystals vary in size, weigh it out)

1 teaspoon **nigella seeds**

1 teaspoon **black mustard seeds**

1 teaspoon **cumin seeds**

½ teaspoon **coriander seeds**

a pinch of **red chilli flakes**

800ml–1-litre sterilized **glass jar with a lid**

TIP

You don't have to have a pickle weight/press to make this kind of pickle, but they are useful for keeping all the veg under the brine and preventing mould forming on the top.

We like this so much we start eating it before we can even get it in the jar. It's perfect served alongside Indian-style curries, with dhal, with poached eggs and garlicky spinach on toast, even inside a cheese toastie...

Mix all the ingredients together in a large bowl and use (clean) hands to massage the salt into the vegetables. Set aside for about 10 minutes.

By now, the vegetables should have started to release some liquid. Pack everything tightly into the sterilized jar, pushing it down with a clean spoon. If the pickle at the top isn't covered with brine, gradually add a little cold water until it is (anything exposed to the air may go mouldy). There should be plenty of head room above the pickle. Seal the lid and leave at a steady room temperature out of direct sunlight. Every day, release the lid to allow any fermenting gases to escape, then re-seal, pushing the pickle under the brine again, if necessary.

When you see tiny bubbles in the brine (this will after at least day, depending on the room's temperature), the pickle may be ready. Taste (use a clean spoon and don't double dip, as this invites mould into the mix) and decide if you would like to leave it longer, or place in the fridge to slow the fermentation. The first time we made this, it was during hot weather and bubbles appeared quickly, but the pickle still needed longer to develop outside the fridge.

Store, sealed and in the fridge, once fermented to your liking. This will keep for up to 6 weeks in the fridge (but ensure you always use clean spoons when taking any out).

HOMEMADE YOGHURT

MAKES 500 ML

PREP TIME: 2 MINS * COOK TIME: 10 MINS PLUS AT LEAST 8 HOURS FERMENTING

WF | GF | V | NF | SoF

500ml **dairy milk**

3 tablespoons **live yoghurt**

Homemade yoghurt is easy to make, very satisfying, incredibly cheap and, especially if you get milk in glass or recyclable packaging, far better for low plastic usage than buying it all the time. You just need one live yoghurt to get you started. Ideally, use a pan thermometer to track the milk's temperature, and make sure everything you use is sparkling clean, otherwise the yoghurt may go off. Full-fat milk gives a thicker, creamier end result, we find.

Set a heavy-based saucepan over a low heat. Slowly and gently, stirring often, heat the milk to 85°C/185°F (almost bubbling). Remove from the heat and allow to cool to 46°C/115°F (just about bearable to the touch).

Meanwhile, bring the live yoghurt up to room temperature. Stir into the cooled milk and then pour the mixture into a thermos flask or tempered glass jar with a lid. Seal loosely, but don't screw the lid on tightly. Wrap in a towel, or place inside a small cool bag, to help keep the warmth inside, as this encourages fermentation. Set aside somewhere where it won't be moved and disturbed, with a steady warmish temperature (the top of a fridge or an airing cupboard) for 8 hours.

After 8 hours, you can begin tasting (always use a clean spoon and don't double dip! You don't want to introduce unwanted bacteria, which could spoil the yoghurt). Once the yoghurt is sour enough, decant into lidded containers or jars, if necessary, and store in the fridge for up to 5 days.

=TIP=

Adding powdered milk gives an even thicker end result. We use about 2 tablespoonfuls for 500ml milk, added when we heat the milk. However, we often don't bother, and if thicker yoghurt is required, we strain the yoghurt using muslin, until rich and creamy.

LABNEH

MAKES 200–250G

PREP TIME: 2 MINS PLUS 8–24 HOURS DRAINING

WF | GF | V | NF | SoF

500g **thick live yoghurt**

Labneh is super-thick yoghurty cheese – sour, tangy and absolutely delicious. You can – and we do – eat it spread on bread with a drizzle of olive oil. Alternatively, serve it in recipes like the courgettes on page 139. We use dairy yoghurt, but you can have a go with dairy-free alternatives, if you like.

Line a colander with some thick muslin or a single layer of pillowcase fabric, then set the colander over a bowl large enough to catch all the whey that will drain from the yoghurt. Pour the yoghurt into the muslin, then cover the whole thing with a plate, to keep out flies and dust.

Set aside and leave to drain for 8–24 hours, depending on how thick your yoghurt is and how firm you like your labneh.

The longer you leave it, the firmer it will get, right up to the point where you will be able to roll it into 3cm balls and store it in a jar of extra virgin olive oil flavoured with garlic and herbs, such as rosemary and thyme.

=TIP=

Don't throw away the leftover liquid – the probiotic whey. You can use it to soak Bircher Muesli (see page 23) or add it to smoothies (page 204) or even dressings, or add it to chicken marinades (it works as a meat tenderizer).

VEGAN YOGHURT

MAKES ABOUT 250ML

PREP TIME: 5 MINS PLUS SOAKING TIME * COOK TIME: 10 MINS

WF | GF | DF | V | Ve | SoF

150g **raw (unroasted) cashews**

100ml cold water

1½ teaspoons **vegan probiotic powder** (including some or all of the following: *lactobacillus acidophilus, bifidobacterium lactis, streptococcus thermophilus, bifidobacterium bifidum*) OR 2 tablesoons **live vegan yoghurt** (choose SoF as needed)

We've experimented with lots of homemade vegan yoghurts, but we think cashews make the best base, as it doesn't need lots of added ingredients like tapioca flour or gums.

Place the cashews in a bowl and cover with some freshly boiled water. Leave to soak for at least 4 hours, or ideally overnight.

Drain and rinse the cashews. Tip them into a powerful blender and add the measured cold water. Blend on high power until completely smooth, adding more water as necessary to get the texture you want – it should be fairly thick.

Pour the cashew mixture into a pan and warm to 37°C/98°F – this is human body temperature, so it should feel just warm to the touch. About 20 seconds in the microwave also does the trick.

Add the probiotic powder or live yoghurt and stir well. Pour the yoghurt into a scrupulously clean, dry jar with a lid, or an insulated thermos flask. Loosely cover with a lid, but don't do it up tightly, and wrap in a towel or place in a small cool bag. Set aside somewhere where it won't be moved and disturbed, with a steady warmish temperature (the top of a fridge or an airing cupboard) for 8–24 hours.

After 8 hours, start tasting. When the yoghurt is tangy enough for you, remove the jar from its warm wrappings and place it in the fridge, to halt the fermentation process. Store, covered, in the fridge for up to 5 days.

═TIP═

Use anywhere you would use traditional yoghurt. For sweet yoghurt, add a splash of maple syrup, date nectar or agave nectar and ½ teaspoon of vanilla extract or vanilla bean paste.

SOURDOUGH BROWNIES WITH A TAHINI SWIRL

MAKES 20 BROWNIES
PREP TIME: 20 MINS * COOK TIME: 30 MINS
V | SoF

150g **dark chocolate** (at least 70% cocoa solids), broken up

50g **unsalted butter**

60ml **rapeseed** or **sunflower oil**

2 **eggs** and 1 **egg white**

a pinch of **fine salt**

100g **caster sugar**

80g **light brown sugar**

at least 3 tablespoons **water**

1 teaspoon **vanilla bean paste**

50g **unsweetened cocoa powder**

120g **sourdough starter** (made with 50:50 water:flour, see page 128)

75g **walnuts**, chopped (optional, omit if NF)

2 tablespoons **tahini**

2 teaspoons **maple syrup**, **honey** or **agave**

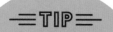

TIP

Add a handful of dried sour cherries, dried blueberries or dried cranberries with the walnuts – their tartness cuts through the chocolate.

Making sourdough (page 128) leaves you with a lot of excess starter that can be used to make crumpets, pancakes or – our favourite – brownies. These are based on a recipe by Izy Hossack. Keep excess starter in a separate jar in the fridge and build it up until you're ready to use it. It will keep for 10 days or more.

Heat the oven to 180°C/350°F/gas mark 4. Line a 20 × 27cm tin with baking paper.

Melt the chocolate, butter and oil in a heatproof bowl set over a pan of just-simmering water until smooth, mixing occasionally. Don't let it overheat. Set aside.

Beat the eggs, egg white, salt and sugar with an electric whisk or stand mixer until pale and moussy (8–10 minutes in a stand mixer; longer with a whisk). Add 2 tablespoons of water and the vanilla and beat for 1–2 minutes.

In a large bowl, stir together the chocolate, cocoa and starter until well combined. Pour into the egg mixture and whisk just until combined. Stir in the walnuts, if using.

Mix the tahini and maple syrup with 1 tablespoon of water, to reach a consistency like honey. The tahini may thicken up at first, but will loosen.

Gently spread the batter into the prepared tin. Drizzle over the tahini mixture in a random pattern, then use a skewer to swirl it to create a marbled effect.

Bake in the oven for 20 minutes (turning the tin after 15 minutes if one side is cooking faster than the other). Insert a skewer into the middle – we like our brownies fudgy but you shouldn't have wet batter on it when you pull it out. If so, bake for a further 2 minutes.

Let cool completely in the tin, then gently remove and slice into 20 pieces.

WATER KEFIR

MAKES 1 LITRE

PREP TIME: 5 MINS PLUS AT LEAST 24 HOURS FERMENTING

WF | GF | DF | V | Ve | NF | SoF

1 litre **water**

50g **sugar** (any kind, but not sugar substitutes, nor honey)

1 tablespoon **unrefined/brown/molasses sugar**

60g **water kefir grains**

½ **unwaxed lemon**

3 × 5mm-thick slices of **fresh ginger**, peeled

3 tablespoons **raisins**, **sultanas** or any **dried fruit**

This is a slightly sparkling (and very slightly alcoholic) drink made with water and sugar. The sugar is mostly fermented away by the living kefir grains (which you will need to buy or be given by a friend) and they generate all sorts of active bacteria for your gut at the same time. The longer you leave the grains to work, the more sour the kefir becomes, so the trick is tasting as you go. If possible, use glass, plastic or wooden utensils to make kefir – it doesn't like contact with metal.

In a perfect world, you make kefir with filtered water, or boiled water left to stand for 24 hours, with organic lemons and un-sulphured dried fruit, because these seem to give kefir the minerals it needs (as does using a bit of unrefined sugar). If you can do all this, you'll undoubtedly have better results and your kefir grains will last longer, too. But don't let not having these things stop you now and then. We sometimes make water kefir with the odd missing link. As long as you stick to the quantities below, you should be okay.

═TIP═

As you make more kefir, your grains will multiply — when this happens, either make more, or give away some. About 3 tablespoons is enough for 1 litre of water.

Pour the water into a glass jar/jug, add the sugar and stir to dissolve. Add all the other ingredients, then cover the jar/jug with a clean cloth or tea towel, and leave somewhere out of direct sunlight, at room temperature, for 24 hours.

Taste – if it's slightly sweet and tangy, then the kefir has got to work. You can strain, bottle and refrigerate it now, or let it keep going for a few more hours. Separate the grains from the spent fruit (we have used the fruit for a second batch, immediately afterwards, too). Every batch will be different depending on the room's temperature.

Store the finished kefir in the fridge for 3–4 days (it will become slightly fizzy if kept in a sealed bottle). The grains can rest for a couple of days in the fridge too, until you're ready to make your next batch.

MILK KEFIR

MAKES 500ML

PREP TIME: 5 MINS PLUS 12–24 HOURS FERMENTING

WF | GF | V | NF | SoF

500ml **whole cows' milk**
2 tablespoons **milk kefir grains**

TIP

You can also use goats' milk to make kefir (we've never tried sheeps' milk, but you could!).

Making milk kefir is very similar to making water kefir, except you need add nothing but milk. You can't make milk kefir with water kefir grains, nor the other way around, so make sure that whatever you buy is the right one for your purposes. We use a couple of tablespoons of milk kefir grains to make our kefir, but you should experiment a bit until you find your sweet spot. Some people find as little as 2 teaspoons is enough for 1 litre of milk.

Use milk kefir anywhere you would use yoghurt, in salad dressings (page 75), smoothies, or make a 50:50 mixture with curd or cream cheese for homemade kefir cheese.

Just as with water kefir, it's best to try to keep contact with metals to the bare minimum or avoid completely by using glass jars or jugs, wooden or plastic spoons, and a plastic strainer.

Put the milk and the milk kefir grains into a large jar/jug and stir together. Cover, either by very loosely screwing on a lid (you need air to circulate) or by covering with a clean tea towel, kitchen paper or muslin and securing with a rubber band or string.

Place somewhere with a steady temperature, ideally warmish, and leave for 24 hours (on really hot days, start to check after 12 hours). Finished kefir means the milk has thickened and it smells tangy, but not too funky.

Strain out the grains, using a sieve, and store the finished kefir in the fridge for 3–4 days (it will become slightly fizzy if kept in a sealed bottle). The grains can rest for a couple of days in the fridge too, until you're ready to make your next batch.

= TIP =

The general advice with kombucha and kefir is to start slowly rather than drinking gallons in a single day. So, even if you love it, build up how much you consume gradually. And remember, if made with black or green tea, it will contain caffeine.

KOMBUCHA

MAKES 1 LITRE

PREP TIME: 2 MINS * COOK TIME: 20 MINS PLUS 4–14 DAYS FERMENTING

WF | GF | DF | V | Ve | NF | SoF

1 litre **water**

3 **tea bags** (we make ours with either **black tea**, **green tea**, **Earl Grey** or **chamomile tea**)

85g **sugar** (not honey)

1 medium **kombucha scoby** (we get ours online from Happy Kombucha)

Kombucha is a fermented tea-based drink – it is now easy to buy ready-made, but we love making it ourselves. Partly, that's because the scoby – the strange gelatinous blob that makes kombucha – is so weird. Formed of a mixture of good bacterias and yeasts, a scoby looks like nothing else – and it ain't pretty – but, when added to a mixture of cold tea and sugar, magic happens. Looked after carefully, a scoby will last a long time and will grow more scobies, too – go online for more info.

Boil the water, then pour into a heatproof container and add the tea bags and sugar. Leave to brew for 20 minutes, then remove the bags and cool the tea.

Your scoby will come in a little pouch or jar with some liquid around it. Once the tea is cold, add the scoby and all the liquid. Cover the container with a clean tea towel, muslin or paper towel (as long as it covers snugly) and secure with a rubber band or string. Set aside, out of direct sunlight, for up to 14 days.

Start tasting after about 4 days, pouring just a little out to taste. The tea will gradually become a little cloudy and, as the sugar is consumed by the scoby, the drink will become tart and almost vinegary. It should no longer taste much like tea, but will become quite complex and a bit fruity. When you're happy with the taste, decant the kombucha into a bottle and store in the fridge.

Keep a little of the kombucha to store the scoby in, so you can add it to your next batch. The longer you keep the finished kombucha, the more likely it is to fizz, so keep releasing the lid of the bottle to avoid a build-up of gas.

Drink chilled over ice or diluted with water.

OMEGA-3

A diet rich in omega-3 fatty acids
means more diverse good
gut bacteria.

SUPER-SEEDED GRANOLA

MAKES ABOUT 12 SERVINGS

PREP TIME: 6 MINS * COOK TIME: 20–30 MINS

WF | DF | V | Ve | SoF

100ml **flavourless oil** (such as **vegetable** or **sunflower oil**)

60ml **maple syrup**

225g **porridge oats** (choose GF if needed)

50g **pumpkin seeds** (or a mixture of **pumpkin** and **sunflower seeds**)

2 tablespoons **ground flaxseeds/linseeds**

150g **mixed nuts: walnuts, Brazil nuts, almonds, hazelnuts** and/or **pecans**, chopped

125g **mixed dried fruit (dates, apricots, prunes** and **mangoes** all contain fibre and prebiotics)

This crunchy granola has a great mix of different fibres with lots of resistant starch in the oats and plentiful prebiotics in the nuts and dried fruit. It cooks to a paler colour than you might expect, because it's lower in sugar.

Preheat the oven to 160°C/325°F/gas mark 3. Lightly grease 2 baking sheets with oil.

Whisk together the oil and maple syrup. Place the oats, seeds and nuts in a large bowl. Pour over half of the maple mixture, then toss. Pour over the rest of the maple mixture and toss again, making sure everything in the bowl gets well coated.

Spread the granola mixture out on the baking sheets and cook in the oven for 10 minutes. Remove and give each mixture a good stir, then return to the oven for another 10–20 minutes, or until the oats and nuts are golden. Remove from the oven and allow to cool.

When completely cool, add the fruit and store in an airtight container for up to 2 weeks.

≡TIP≡

Granola isn't just for mornings – we like it on yoghurty desserts, too.

≡TIP≡

If any of your frozen
berries are large, chop
them into small pieces, or
they will sink and leak lots
of juice into the muffins as
they cook.

FRUIT & FLAXSEED MUFFINS

MAKES 10 MUFFINS

PREP TIME: 15 MINS ✱ COOK TIME: 30–35 MINS

V | SoF

2 tablespoons **ground flaxseeds/linseeds**

2 tablespoons **water**

75ml **very mild-tasting extra virgin olive oil** (if you don't have a mild version, use **flavourless vegetable oil** instead)

175ml **milk** (any kind, can be DF/Ve, as needed)

1 teaspoon **raw, unpasteurized apple cider vinegar** (with mother)

zest of ½ **lemon**

250g **plain flour**

1½ teaspoons **baking powder**

½ teaspoon **bicarbonate of soda**

a pinch of **salt**

125g **caster sugar**

2 tablespoons **ground almonds**

125g **frozen berries**

1 tablespoon **demerara sugar**, for sprinkling (optional)

Flaxseeds are a good source of plant-based omega-3, especially important if you have a plant-based diet. Often, they're soaked in water and used as binder, instead of eggs, as we've done here. This is a spin on the vegan blueberry muffin recipe we created for our book 'Fast Vegan', but using mixed frozen berries to make it a year-round recipe (use fresh blueberries when in season).

Preheat the oven to 190°C/375°F/gas mark 5. Line a muffin tin with 10 paper cases.

Mix the flaxseeds with the water in a small bowl and leave to soak for 5 minutes.

Whisk together the oil, milk, vinegar and lemon zest.

Sift the flour, baking powder and bicarbonate of soda together in a large bowl. Add the salt and sugar and mix thoroughly. Add the ground almonds and frozen berries and mix again (coating the berries in flour makes them less likely to sink). Add the oil and flaxseed mixtures to the bowl and stir until just combined – it doesn't need to be perfectly smooth and over-mixing will smash the fruit and make the muffins claggy.

Divide the mixture between the paper cases and sprinkle with the demerara sugar, if using. Bake in the oven for 30–35 minutes. When done, the tops should be light golden and firm, and a skewer inserted into the middle should come out clean.

Leave to cool in the tin for 5–10 minutes, then turn out and cool on a rack.

These are best eaten the same day they are made (or frozen once cool) but will keep in an airtight container for a couple of days.

SMOKED FISH WITH KEFIR & DILL

SERVES 2

PREP TIME: 5 MINS

NF | SoF

butter, for spreading

2 slices of **wholegrain sourdough bread**, toasted, or 4 slices of **rye bread**

2 tablespoons **cream cheese**

2 tablespoons **milk kefir**

2 fillets **hot-smoked fish (mackerel** or **trout)**, skin removed, flaked, or 4–8 slices **smoked salmon**

freshly squeezed **lemon juice**, to taste

leaves from 2–3 sprigs of **dill**

freshly ground black pepper, to taste

Gut-healthy food doesn't have to be complicated, as demonstrated by this super simple recipe.

If your milk kefir is thick enough to spread, use 4 tablespoonfuls of it and no cream cheese. Alternatively, you can buy kefir and cream cheese ready mixed – it's called kefir cheese – in supermarkets and wholefood stores.

Butter the toast or bread. Mix together the cream cheese and kefir, then spread on top of the butter. Arrange the fish on top and squeeze over a little lemon juice. Scatter over the dill and finish with a few twists of black pepper.

TIP

Turn this into a little canapé by serving on top of crackers, such as the Rye Crackers on page 71. Alternatively, top each open sandwich with another slice of bread, for a picnic.

=TIP=

If you don't eat eggs, you can use aquafaba, the gloopy liquid in a can of chickpeas, to coat the fish – just make sure it's fairly thick (if not, reduce it on the hob).

SALMON FISH FINGER SANDWICH WITH ANCHOVY MAYO

SERVES 4

PREP TIME: 8 MINS * COOK TIME: 16 MINS

DF | NF | SoF

1–2 **eggs**

a splash of **milk** (any kind)

4 tablespoons **gluten-free plain flour**

100g **ready-made, gluten-free breadcrumbs**

2 tablespoons **extra virgin olive oil**, plus more as needed

400–450g **wild sockeye salmon**, skin removed, sliced into 3cm-wide fingers

salt and **freshly ground black pepper**

FOR THE MAYO:

4 heaped tablespoons **mayonnaise**

4 **anchovies** (or more, to taste), finely chopped

zest and juice of ½ **lemon**

freshly ground black pepper

TO SERVE:

8 slices **toasted wholemeal bread** or **sourdough** (can be WF/GF) or 4 warmed **wholegrain wraps**

freshly squeezed lemon juice

crispy lettuce

cucumber slices

We love gluten-free breadcrumbs. Mostly made from rice flour, we find they crunch up better and are less likely to burn than wheat-based crumbs.

Sockeye is a firmer, redder salmon than you might be used to, high in omega-3 and often a more sustainable option than other farmed or wild salmons. If you don't want a sarnie, serve these fish fingers with some green vegetables.

Mix all the ingredients for the mayo in a bowl until well combined. Set aside.

Beat 1 egg in a bowl (save the other – you may not need it) and stir in a splash of milk. Place a couple of tablespoons of flour into another bowl and season with salt and pepper. Tip the breadcrumbs into a third bowl.

Set a wide frying pan over a medium heat. When hot, cover the base with oil. Working briskly, dip the salmon into the flour, then the egg, letting the excess drain away, and then the breadcrumbs. Be sure every finger is well covered in each layer.

Fry each fish finger in the hot oil for about 2 minutes or until golden on the bottom, then turn gently, cooking each side briefly for maximum crunch. Repeat until all the fish fingers are cooked, adding more oil to the pan, or more coatings to the bowls, as needed. Keep the cooked fish fingers warm while you cook the rest.

Spread the bottom half of each sandwich with the anchovy mayo and place 3–4 fish fingers on top. Squeeze over a little lemon juice and finish with some lettuce, cucumber and the top slice of toast/bread. Alternatively, roll into wraps.

MACKEREL PÂTÉ & BEETROOT TARTINES

SERVES 4 AS A STARTER OR WITH OTHER DISHES (MAKES 12)

PREP TIME: 10 MINS

WF | NF | SoF

1 small **beetroot** (about 75g), trimmed, very thinly sliced, then cut into strips

a little **freshly squeezed lemon juice**

3 slices **German-style 3-grain rye bread**, cut into 3 rectangles

FOR THE MACKEREL PÂTÉ:

125g **smoked mackerel**, skin removed, flaked

1 heaped tablespoon **Homemade Crème Fraîche** (see Tip, page 195) or **sour cream** (use **vegan mayonnaise** or **vegan crème fraîche** if DF)

1 teaspoon finely chopped **chives**

1 tablespoon finely chopped **dill**

1 teaspoon **freshly squeezed lemon juice**, or to taste

freshly ground black pepper, to taste

Tartines is just a posh and rather lovely word for little open sandwiches. You could serve these at a party, or keep them all to yourself and have them for lunch.

If you don't have or like beetroot, thin slices of cucumber are a great alternative.

To make the mackerel pâté, mix together the flaked mackerel, crème fraîche, herbs, lemon juice and black pepper in a bowl. Taste and add more pepper or lemon juice, if you like.

Toss the beetroot strips in a little lemon juice.

Pile each rectangle of rye bread with the mackerel pâté, then top with the beetroot. Tuck in.

=TIP=

Try using hot-smoked fish, such as trout or salmon, or use finely chopped cold-smoked salmon, instead. In a pinch, it even works with canned salmon (although canned has lower amounts of omega-3).

CELERIAC, APPLE & SMOKED MACKEREL SALAD

½ small **celeriac** (175g), peeled and sliced into matchsticks

1 tart **eating apple** (like a **Granny Smith**), peeled, cored and sliced into matchsticks

freshly squeezed lemon juice

2–3 **smoked mackerel fillets** (150–200g), skin removed, flaked

FOR THE DRESSING:

3 tablespoons **extra virgin olive oil**

1 teaspoon **freshly squeezed lemon juice**

1 teaspoon **wholegrain mustard**

½ teaspoon **honey**

2 tablespoons **Homemade Crème Fraîche** (see Tip, page 195) (optional)

a pinch of **salt** and some **freshly ground black pepper**

We happened to have some leftover Homemade Crème Fraîche (see Tip, page 195) lying around when we were working on this recipe, so we tipped a bit into the bowl, on a whim. While not essential, it does do something rather magical to an already lovely salad. If you don't do dairy, try vegan mayo, or leave it out completely.

Celariac contains different types of fibres, while smoked mackerel is a great source of omega-3.

Place the sliced celeriac and apple in a large bowl and squeeze over some lemon juice, then toss to coat (this helps prevent them turning brown). Add the flaked mackerel and toss again.

Whisk together all the dressing ingredients. If the crème fraîche makes it very, very thick, add a little water to thin, but go steady – you don't want to make the dish sloppy.

Add half of the dressing to the salad bowl and toss. Add more dressing as needed.

Eat immediately, or keep in the fridge for up to 2 days (bring up to room temperature before serving).

≡TIP≡

It sounds odd, but a few torn-up mint leaves are a delicious addition. If that's too much for you, go for watercress, instead. Not keen on apple? Swap it for finely sliced orange.

CRAB, WATERCRESS & MANGO SALAD

SERVES 2 AS A MAIN COURSE OR 4 AS A STARTER

PREP TIME: 10 MINS ★ COOK TIME: 5 MINS

WF | GF | NF | SoF

80g **fine green beans**, cut in half

60g **watercress**

4 **spring onions**, thinly sliced

150g **white crab meat**

½ large ripe **mango**, cut into 2cm chunks

salt and **freshly ground black pepper**, to taste

extra virgin olive oil, to serve

FOR THE DRESSING:

3 tablespoons **crème fraîche** (homemade if you like, see Tip, page 195)

1 tablespoon **wholegrain mustard**

1 **lime**: ½ juiced; ½ cut into wedges, to serve

1 tablespoon finely chopped **dill**

1 tablespoon finely chopped **chives**

salt and **freshly ground black pepper**, to taste

A light and tasty salad, with omega-3-rich crab. Don't be afraid to use fruit in a savoury setting. The combination of mango and fish is amazing, and mango has been shown in a few studies to be good for general gut health, probably due to its combination of polyphenols and prebiotic fibres.

Cook the green beans in a pan of boiling water for 2 minutes. Immediately drain, transfer to a bowl of ice-cold water to cool, then drain again. Set aside.

To make the dressing, combine the crème fraîche, mustard, lime juice, dill and chives together in a small bowl. Add salt and pepper to taste.

In a large mixing bowl, combine the cooked beans, watercress, spring onions, crab meat and mango. Add most of the dressing, saving a little bit to drizzle over at the end. Mix until well combined. Taste for seasoning and acidity, adding salt, pepper and lime juice, to your taste.

Divide between bowls, spoon over the remaining dressing and drizzle over some extra virgin olive oil. Serve with lime wedges.

≡TIP≡

Nectarines or peaches work really well in this, too. If it's not the season, try apples or grapes. If you don't have watercress, rocket will be fine.

MISO-CRUSTED SALMON WITH BLACK RICE & CUCUMBER PICKLE

SERVES 4

PREP TIME: 10 MINS * COOK TIME: 40 MINS

WF | DF | NF

220g **black rice**

1 teaspoon **mirin** (or a pinch of sugar)

1 tablespoon **miso paste**

1 teaspoon **soy sauce/tamari** (use GF if needed), plus extra to serve

4 **salmon fillets** (about 120g each, try to use wild rather than farmed salmon)

125g **frozen edamame beans**

a pinch of **black** or **white sesame seeds**, or a mixture, to serve

toasted sesame oil, to serve

FOR THE CUCUMBER PICKLE:

125g **cucumber**, sliced into long thin ribbons

a really generous pinch of **sugar**

a generous pinch of **salt**

a pinch of **black** or **white sesame seeds**, or a mixture

½ teaspoon **rice vinegar** or **raw, unpasteurized apple cider vinegar** (with mother)

1 teaspoon very finely grated **fresh ginger**

This has so much going for it: omegas from the salmon and sesame oil and an explosion of fibre and polyphenols from the black rice and edamame. Also, it looks pretty and tastes fabulous.

Place the rice in a pan with a lid (use a pan that won't stain), cover with cold water, and bring to a simmer over a medium heat. Cook until tender, up to 35 minutes. Drain any excess water, fluff up with a fork and cover with the lid until ready to serve.

Meanwhile, thoroughly mix the mirin, miso paste and soy sauce/tamari together, then rub the mixture all over the salmon fillets. Set aside.

Mix all the cucumber pickle ingredients together in a small bowl, and set aside.

Once the rice is cooked, heat the grill to medium.

Place the beans in a pan of boiling water, bring back to the boil and simmer for a couple of minutes. Drain and keep warm.

When the grill is hot, grill the salmon, skin-side up, for 2 minutes. Cook until dark but not scorched (the marinade can easily burn), then turn the salmon and cook the other side for 3–4 minutes, or until the salmon is just cooked through and beginning to flake. Don't allow it to overcook and fall apart.

Serve in wide bowls, with the rice on the bottom, the edamame beans and salmon on top, and the cucumber pickle alongside. Finish with a drizzle of toasted sesame oil and extra soy sauce on the table.

=TIP=

For an easy lunch, cook an
extra portion or two of the
salmon and store in the
fridge, to eat with the Sour
Thai-style Salad (see page 91)
the next day.

SPANISH SPICED WHOLE MACKEREL

SERVES 4

PREP TIME: 10 MINS * COOK TIME: 22–25 MINS

WF | GF | DF | NF | SoF

4 **whole mackerel** (about 300–350g each), gutted and cleaned

2 **lemons**: 1 thinly sliced; 1 halved for squeezing

extra virgin olive oil, for drizzling

salt and **freshly ground black pepper**

FOR THE SPICE PASTE:

4 cloves of **garlic**, peeled

a pinch of **salt**

2 teaspoons **sweet paprika**

1 teaspoon **ground cumin**

a small handful of **flat-leaf parsley leaves**, roughly chopped, plus extra to serve

a small handful of **dill**, roughly chopped

2 tablespoons **extra virgin olive oil**

generous grinding of **freshly ground black pepper**

≡TIP≡

If you can't find fresh whole mackerel, this recipe can be used to cook other oily fish, such as salmon and trout.

Fresh mackerel is full of flavour and omega-3s. This simple technique – wrapping the fish in foil before baking – gives impressive results. A crisp slaw with fennel and cucumber (see page 111 for slaw basics) is just right with this.

Heat the oven to 180°C/350°F/gas mark 4.

To make the spice paste, in a pestle and mortar, smash the garlic cloves with the salt until a paste starts to form. Add the paprika, cumin, pepper, parsley and dill and pound until you have a thick, fragrant paste. Add the extra virgin olive oil to loosen it up and stir to combine.

Lay out a piece of kitchen foil large enough to wrap all 4 fish up like a parcel. Pat each fish dry, inside and out, with some kitchen paper. Season the insides and outsides generously with salt and pepper, then stuff the cavities with a few slices of lemon and some of the spice paste. Drizzle with more olive oil and the remaining spice paste, then fold the foil to form a parcel around the fish, making a tight seal at the top to trap the steam. Place in a large roasting tray and bake for 22–25 mins, depending on the size of the fish. You can peek in to check if the fish is done – the flesh should be firm and just beginning to flake.

Open up the foil parcel, divide the fish between 4 plates and spoon over any juices left in the tray or foil. Squeeze over a generous amount of lemon juice and garnish with some fresh parsley.

OMEGA-3

ORECCHIETTE PASTA WITH KALE, WATERCRESS & PISTACHIO PESTO

SERVES 2 AS A MAIN COURSE OR 4 AS A STARTER
PREP TIME: 15 MINS * COOK TIME: 15 MINS
V | SoF

50g **shelled, roasted, unsalted pistachios**

15g **watercress**, thick stems removed

35g **kale** or **cavolo nero**, middle ribs removed

zest and juice of ½ **lemon** (keep the other half in case you want to add more), to taste

1 **ice cube** (this will keep the pesto an electric green colour)

120ml **extra virgin olive oil**, plus extra (optional) to preserve the pesto or serve

50g **Parmesan cheese**, freshly grated, plus extra to serve

250g **orecchiette pasta**

salt and **freshly ground black pepper**, to taste

A gut-friendly version of classic Genovese pesto, with extra greenery for both flavour and nutrients. The watercress and kale add a lovely pepperiness, offset by the lemon and garlic. The pistachios keep everything an eye-catching vivid green. We like orecchiette pasta here because it holds the pesto well.

Combine the pistachios, watercress, kale, lemon zest and juice, ice cube and half of the olive oil in a blender or food processor. Pulse a few times, then blend on a low setting to thoroughly combine. With the blades running slowly, gradually pour in the remaining oil through the feed tube until well blended. Add the Parmesan and blend to combine. Taste and season with salt and pepper to taste. Add a splash more lemon juice if you think it needs it. Scrape into a bowl and set aside. If making in advance, cover the pesto with a thin layer of olive oil to prevent oxidization.

Cook the pasta in a pan of heavily salted boiling water for 1 minute less than the packet instructions. Drain, reserving a mugful of the pasta water.

Return the pasta to the pan but don't return it to the heat. Stir in the pesto (you probably won't need it all – just enough to coat everything). Add a splash of pasta water to loosen it up – the starchiness in the water will also help bind the sauce to the pasta. Stir for a minute or so until everything has emulsified and the pesto is clinging to the pasta. If the mixture is a bit thick, add more pasta water little by little.

Serve in bowls, sprinkled with a bit of Parmesan and a little olive oil. Crack over some fresh black pepper and eat immediately.

=TIP=

Try to find a good-quality bronze-dyed pasta. It isn't that much more expensive, but the slightly rougher texture means that the sauce clings to the pasta.

=TIP=

Fresh sardines can be used here too – add at the same time as for canned, but allow to cook through in the pan.

SICILIAN SARDINE PASTA

SERVES 4

PREP TIME: 8 MINS * COOK TIME: 25 MINS

DF | SoF

4 tablespoons **extra virgin olive oil**, for
    cooking

1 slice of **day-old bread**, ideally
    sourdough, crusts removed and
    chopped or torn into crumbs

1 **onion**, very finely chopped

½ head of **fennel**, finely chopped, fronds
    separated and reserved

a generous pinch of **fennel seeds**

3 **anchovies**

2 cloves of **garlic**, crushed

500g **fresh egg tagliatelle** or 400g **dried
    tagliatelle**, **spaghetti** or **linguine**

3 tablespoons **pine nuts**

a pinch of **saffron threads**

2 tablespoons **raisins** or **sultanas**

2 × 128g cans **sardines in oil**, drained

salt and **freshly ground black pepper**

2 tablespoons finely chopped **flat-leaf
    parsley**, to serve

extra virgin olive oil, to serve

*Rebecca first tasted this amazing combination in Sicily, where it would usually
be made with fresh sardines. It's got the lot: omega-3 from the fish, prebiotics
from the onion, fennel and dried fruit, and polyphenols from the oil. You can use
any kind of pasta, but it goes beautifully with Gram Flour Pasta (page 37).*

Heat 2 tablespoons of the olive oil in a wide frying pan over a medium heat. Add the
breadcrumbs and cook, stirring, until golden brown and crispy. Remove from the
pan with a slotted spoon and set aside. Ensure no crumbs remain in the pan.

Add another tablespoon of olive oil to the pan, then add the onion and fennel.
Gently cook for about 10 minutes until soft and translucent, but not brown (reduce
the heat if necessary). Add the fennel seeds, anchovies and garlic and cook, stirring,
until the anchovies dissolve and the garlic no longer smells raw.

If you are cooking dried pasta, put it in a pan of salted boiling water while the
anchovies are cooking and cook for 1 minute less than the packet instructions. If
cooking fresh pasta, wait until after the pine nuts are cooked.

Heat the final tablespoon of oil in a small pan over a low heat. Add the pine nuts and
toast until golden all over, then remove from the pan.

Stir the saffron and raisins/sultanas into the sauce. Just before serving, add the
sardines and gently stir them in, breaking them up a little, but not mashing them.

Drain the pasta, reserving a little of the water. Toss the pasta, breadcrumbs,
pine nuts and sauce together with a little black pepper. If it looks dry, add 1–2
tablespoons of the reserved pasta water. Serve sprinkled with parsley and drizzled
with just a little extra virgin olive oil.

=TIP=

Not into beef?
Use crispy tofu,
grilled fish, or even
prawns, instead.

SEARED BEEF & GRAIN SALAD WITH CHILLI, CORIANDER & MINT

SERVES 2

PREP TIME: 20 MINS ∗ COOK TIME: 30 MINS

DF

FOR THE SALAD:

225g grass-fed **rump steak**

20g each of **spelt grain**, **brown rice** and **buckwheat**

50g raw **snap peas** or **mange tout**, sliced into 2cm pieces

75g **green beans**, raw or blanched

75g **tenderstem broccoli**, raw or blanched, stems cut into 5cm slices

1 **spring onion**, cut into 2cm pieces

100g **cucumber**, sliced into thin strips

leaves from 3 sprigs of **mint**, torn if large

a generous handful of **coriander leaves**

flavourless oil, for cooking

2 tablespoons chopped **roasted peanuts**

FOR THE DRESSING:

2 tablespoons **fish sauce**

zest of ¼ **lime**

3 tablespoons **freshly squeezed lime juice**

1 teaspoon **flavourless oil** (like **rapeseed**)

1 teaspoon **toasted sesame oil**

½ teaspoon **soy sauce/tamari**

½ teaspoon **honey**

1cm piece of **ginger**, peeled, finely grated

1 clove of **garlic**, crushed

½–1 **red chilli**, deseeded, finely chopped

We don't think all meat is bad, but making more room for gut-friendly foods inevitably leaves less room for meat. But beef does contain omega-3 fatty acids. If possible, choose grass-fed beef which has been pastured and farmed responsibly (without the potential for gut-flora-damaging extra antibiotics).

Remove the steak from the fridge and leave to come up to room temperature.

Place the spelt grain and brown rice in a pan and cover with water. Bring to the boil, cover with a lid, reduce to a simmer and cook for 5 minutes. Add the buckwheat to the pan and cook for a further 15 minutes. Drain and tip onto a plate to cool.

Meanwhile, prepare all the salad vegetables and herbs and place everything in a large bowl. Stir together the dressing ingredients with 1 tablespoon of cold water in a small bowl.

Place a heavy-based frying pan over a high heat. When it is really hot, add a splash of cooking oil, swirling it around to coat the base. Add the steak and cook for 2 minutes until well browned, then turn and cook the other side (the steak should be quite rare). Remove from the pan and set aside to rest for 5 minutes.

Add the cooled grains to the salad bowl, then add half of the dressing and toss.

Slice the rested steak into 5mm-thick pieces, cutting against the grain of the meat. Dress the meat with a quarter of the remaining dressing.

Divide the salad between 2 plates, then top with the steak and peanuts. Serve with the remaining dressing on the side and eat immediately.

OMEGA SPRINKLES

MAKES 4–6 SERVINGS

PREP TIME: 1 MINS

WF | GF | DF | V | Ve | NF | SoF

1 tablespoon **ground flaxseeds/linseeds**

2 tablespoons **pumpkin seeds**

3 tablespoons **sunflower seeds**

1 tablespoon **toasted sesame seeds** (or use a mixture of **black** and **white toasted sesame seeds**)

1 tablespoon **hulled hemp seeds** (or choose **roasted hemp seeds**)

=TIP=

Turn this into something like trail mix by adding nuts, dried fruit and maybe even some chopped-up polyphenol-rich dark chocolate.

The seeds in this sprinkle are all good sources of fatty acids, as well as fibre. As long as our flax seeds are already ground (we buy them that way), we tend to just mix the rest of the seeds together, giving maximum crunch when we sprinkle them onto yoghurt, Bircher Muesli (see page 23), porridge or over salads. However, if you like, you can give them a rough grind, either in a pestle and mortar or a spice grinder, for a slightly finer texture. For a toastier flavour, roast in a low oven (150°C/300°F/gas mark 2) for 10 minutes or until nutty.

Eating too much flax without enough liquid can be unpleasant, or upset your tummy, which is why we recommend this as a sprinkle, or added to a snack – don't overdo it.

Mix everything together, then store in a sealed container. Use within 2 weeks.

FLAX OIL SALAD DRESSING

MAKES ENOUGH TO DRESS 1 GREEN SALAD

PREP TIME: 4 MINS

WF | GF | DF | V | Ve | NF | SoF

1 teaspoon **raw, unpasteurized apple cider vinegar** (with mother) (check Ve if necessary)

a pinch of **sea salt**

1 tablespoon **Dijon mustard** (check Ve if necessary)

¼–½ teaspoon **honey** or **maple syrup**, or more to taste (use **maple syrup** if Ve)

1 tablespoon **extra virgin olive oil**

1 tablespoon **virgin cold-pressed flaxseed oil**

1 tablespoon **water**

freshly squeezed lemon juice (optional)

Flax oil is rich in plant-based omega-3 fatty acids, but can be bitter, depending on the brand, so we usually combine it with a good-quality extra virgin olive oil.

You can make a nice dressing with just 1 tablespoon extra virgin olive oil, 1 tablespoon virgin cold-pressed flaxseed oil, 1 teaspoon live apple cider vinegar (with mother) and a pinch of sea salt, all whisked together. But if we want something more French, for bitter leaves such as chicory or watercress, or a dressing that will stand up to some blue cheese or toasted walnuts, we go for this one.

Combine the vinegar, salt, mustard and honey or maple syrup in a small bowl and stir until smooth. Mix the oils together, then slowly add to the mustard mixture, stirring all the time. After a bit of vigorous mixing, you should get a smooth emulsion. It will be quite thick, so thin with about a tablespoon of water, until you get a pourable, but not watery, dressing. Taste – if your vinegar is quite sweet you won't need more sugar but you might feel a bit of lemon juice would be good. If the vinegar is very sour, you may want to add a tiny bit more sweetness. Check the salt levels, too.

Serve immediately, or it will keep in the fridge, covered, for at least 3–4 days.

═TIP═

You can use this 50:50 mixture of oils whenever you would normally use olive oil in a dressing. Try omitting the mustard, or using wholegrain, but adding finely chopped soft green herbs: parsley, basil, tarragon or chives, depending on the kind of salad you want to serve it with.

LOWER SUGAR
(BUT STILL SWEET)

Too much sugar can upset our
gut's microbial balance.

CHOCOLATE BEETROOT CAKE

SERVES 6

PREP TIME: 40 MINS * COOK TIME: 30 MINS

V | NF | SoF

FOR THE CAKE:

150g good-quality **dark chocolate** (70% cocoa solids): 100g melted; 50g roughly chopped

250g **beetroot**, peeled, cooked and roughly chopped

2 tablespoons **mild olive oil**

125ml **flavourless rapeseed** or **sunflower oil**

125g **caster sugar**

2 teaspoons **vanilla bean paste**

a pinch of **salt**

4 free-range **eggs**, separated

50g good-quality **cocoa powder**

150g **plain flour**

2 teaspoons **baking powder**

3–4 tablespoons **fruit compote**

FOR THE GANACHE FROSTING:

75g good-quality **dark chocolate** (70% cocoa solids), melted

¼ teaspoon **vanilla bean paste**

1 teaspoon **caster sugar**

2 tablespoons thick and creamy **full-fat Greek-style live yoghurt**

No one we tested this cake on realized it contained three whole (polyphenol-rich) beetroot, as well as gut-friendly dark chocolate. Because it has relatively little added sugar, it can taste a little austere without the ganache, which we make with live yoghurt instead of the usual cream.

Heat the oven to 175°C/350°F/gas mark 4. Grease and line two 20cm springform cake tins.

Combine the melted chocolate, beetroot, oils, sugar, vanilla bean paste and salt in a food processor and blitz until smooth, scraping down the sides with a spatula once or twice. Add the egg yolks and blitz very briefly, just enough to mix.

In a separate bowl, beat the egg whites just until white and moussy.

Sift the cocoa, flour and baking powder into a large mixing bowl. Add the beetroot mixture and egg whites to the dry ingredients along with the chopped chocolate, and fold together until just combined.

Pour the batter into the prepared tins and bake in the oven for 30 minutes, or until a skewer inserted into the middle comes out clean. Leave to cool in the tins for 15 minutes before placing on a rack to cool completely.

When cooled, sandwich the cakes together with the fruit compote.

To make the ganache, beat all the ingredients together until completely smooth and uniform in colour. Working quickly, before it firms up, spread over the top of the cake. Set aside at least until the ganache is set, before serving.

=TIP=

For reasons we can't entirely explain, beetroot cake is much better the day after it's first cooked. Because the beetroot makes it quite fudgy, it keeps well, too.

BERRY, ORANGE & CANNELLINI BEAN CAKE

SERVES 8

PREP TIME: 10 MINS ✳ COOK TIME: 45–50 MINS

WF | GF | V | SoF

75g **unsalted butter**

400g **canned cannellini beans** in water, drained

100g **ground almonds**

3 **eggs**

125g **soft brown sugar**

2 teaspoons **vanilla bean paste**

½ teaspoon **bicarbonate of soda**

1 teaspoon **baking powder**

zest of 1 small **orange** (unwaxed if possible)

125g **mixed frozen berries**

2 tablespoons **flaked almonds**

thick and creamy live yoghurt, to serve

Rebecca's first experience of baking with pulses was making delicate and sweet little chickpea tarts when she was working in Lisbon, a traditional recipe with which she still enjoys confusing her friends. So far, in six years of blind tasting, no one has ever guessed what their mystery ingredient is. Here, the beans are blitzed into the batter, replacing both the flour and much of the fat usually required in a cake. Like most of our desserts in this book, we've reduced the usual amount of sugar used in a cake – we don't think you will taste the difference. And you certainly won't taste the beans, either.

Heat the oven to 190°C/375°F/gas mark 5. Grease and line a deep 20cm springform cake tin.

Place the butter, cannellini beans, ground almonds, eggs, sugar, vanilla bean paste, bicarbonate of soda, baking powder and orange zest into a food processor and blitz until no trace of the beans are visible. The final texture, because of the ground almonds, should be like hummus, but not at all gritty. If in doubt, blitz some more.

Pour the mixture in the prepared tin. Scatter 100g of the fruit over the cake and gently press it into the batter with a spoon – don't stir, though, or the cake will turn purple. Arrange the rest of the fruit randomly on top of the cake. Scatter over the flaked almonds, pressing in gently but leaving most visible.

Bake in the oven for 45–50 minutes, or until the top is a deep golden brown and a skewer inserted into the middle comes out clean. Leave to cool in the tin before serving.

TIP

This is a very adaptable cake: swap flaked almonds for chopped hazelnuts; use fresh berries, or frozen blueberries, or dried fruit, or stoned and chopped plums; or don't use fruit at all; use lemon zest instead of orange.

PEAR FRANGIPANE

SERVES 12
PREP TIME: 10 MINS * COOK TIME: 30–40 MINS
V | SoF

50g **unsalted butter**, melted, plus extra
  for greasing
6 sheets **filo pastry** (approx 20 × 30cm)
3 **pears**, cored and cut into 6 long
  segments
live yoghurt or **Homemade Crème Fraîche**
  (see Tip, page 195), to serve

FOR THE FRANGIPANE FILLING:
3 **eggs**, beaten
125g **caster sugar**
175g **ground almonds**
50g **butter**, softened
½ teaspoon **vanilla bean paste**
1 tablespoon **plain flour**

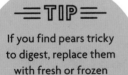
=TIP=
If you find pears tricky
to digest, replace them
with fresh or frozen
berries instead.

We were happy to discover we could use as little as 10g added sugar per slice in this traditional almond pudding, without it feeling like a compromise. Pears (especially the skins) are rich in fibre while almonds contain prebiotics that feed our gut bacteria. Filo is a healthier alternative to regular pastry and you can get away with using slightly less, too, reducing the amount of refined carbs.

Heat the oven to 180°C/350°F/gas mark 4. Lightly grease a 23cm springform tart tin with butter.

Place a pastry sheet on a board (keep the rest covered with a damp tea towel so they don't dry out). Brush the sheet with butter, then lie it across the tin so that one short side overhangs the edge. Gently crumple and tuck it inside the rim of the tin, to begin forming a frilly crust. Brush another sheet with butter, then place it so it half covers the first sheet. Rumple up the overhanging pastry as before. Repeat until all 6 sheets are used up. Brush the frilly rim gently with a little more butter. Bake the tart shell in the oven for 10–15 minutes, until light gold and just crisp.

Meanwhile, blitz together the eggs, sugar, almonds, butter and vanilla bean paste in a food processor. Once smooth, stir in the flour.

When the tart shell is ready, remove from the oven and pour in the filling. Arrange the pear slices on top. Return the tart to the oven and bake for 20–25 minutes until the filling is golden brown. Check after 10 minutes – if it is cooking unevenly, rotate the tin to make sure it colours all over.

Cool in the tin before serving either warm or at room temperature with a dollop of live yoghurt or crème fraîche.

BLUEBERRY GALETTE

SERVES 8

PREP TIME: 10 MINS PLUS CHILLING TIME   *   COOK TIME: 55–65 MINS

V | NF | SoF

FOR THE PASTRY:

50g **wholemeal flour**

150g **plain white spelt flour**

1 tablespoon **sugar**

125g **slightly salted butter**, cubed and
   chilled in the freezer before use

¼ teaspoon **fine salt** (omit if your butter is
   very salty)

1–2 tablespoons **ice-cold water**

FOR THE EGG WASH:

1 **egg**, beaten

splash of **milk**

FOR THE FILLING:

200g **blueberries**

1 tablespoon **plain white spelt flour**

1 tablespoon **caster sugar**

2 teaspoons **demerara** or **golden
   granulated sugar**

about 1 tablespoon **butter**, in small pieces

Homemade Crème Fraîche (see Tip,
   opposite) or **thick yoghurt**, to serve

Not all puddings have to be loaded with sugar – this has far less sugar than many others, getting the rest of its sweetness from fruit (which also lends us fibre and colourful polyphenols). Galettes are free-form tarts and very easy to put together.

Touch the dough as little as possible – the butter will melt and ruin the texture of the pastry. If it gets too warm at any point, and becomes tacky or greasy, whizz it straight back into the fridge for 10 minutes.

Place all the pastry ingredients, except the water, into a food processor and blitz until the mixture looks like sand. Tip the mix into a bowl and add 1 tablespoon of the water – this may be enough to bring the dough together. Working briskly, form a ball of dough with your hands. It should be firm and just holding together – don't add so much water that it becomes sticky.

Flatten the ball to form a thick disc. Place in a bowl and cover with a tea towel, or wrap in clingfilm, and chill in the fridge for 30 minutes.

When ready to cook, heat the oven to 180°C/350°F/gas mark 4.

Beat together the egg and milk for the egg wash.

Place a sheet of baking paper, large enough to take a 25cm disc, onto a work surface. Remove the dough from the fridge and roll it out, directly onto the paper, to form a rough disc about 25cm across and 2–3mm thick – it doesn't matter if the edges are a bit ragged. It will almost certainly warm up a bit, so pop it back into the fridge for 10 minutes, if so.

LOWER SUGAR (BUT STILL SWEET)

Remove from the fridge and transfer the dough to a baking sheet, still on the paper. Brush the pastry disc all over with egg wash. Toss the blueberries with the flour and caster sugar, then tip them into the middle of the pastry. Arrange in a single layer, leaving a gap of 5–6cm all the way round. Gently fold the remaining pastry inwards, partly covering the fruit around the edges, pleating the pastry where necessary. Brush the newly exposed pastry with egg wash, using the wash to help pinch together and seal any cracks in the bottom or sides of the pastry. Sprinkle the pastry with the demerara/granulated sugar. Finally, dot the fruit with the butter.

Bake in the oven for 35–45 minutes, but start checking on it at about 30 minutes. The top should steadily turn golden brown, but the base will take longer to cook (no one wants a soggy bottom). If necessary, use a spatula to very, very gently lift the tart and check the pastry underneath. If the top seems to be darkening too quickly, cover with a sheet of foil for the last few minutes of cooking. Don't worry if some fruit juice bursts through the pastry in places – the charm of this tart is its rustic rough-and-readiness.

Once cooked, remove from the oven and leave to cool on the baking sheet.

Gently slide the galette off the paper and onto a flat surface or plate to serve. Slice and serve warm or at room temperature with crème fraîche or thick yoghurt.

≡ TIP ≡

To make crème fraiche, stir 2 of tablespoons of live yoghurt into 300ml of cream. Leave, covered, at room temperature for 12–24 hours. When it's thickened noticeably and tangy to taste, it's ready. Store, covered, in the fridge, for about 5 days.

TARTINE'S SALTED CHOCOLATE RYE COOKIES

MAKES 18–20 COOKIES

PREP TIME: 15 MINS, PLUS 20 MINS CHILLING ＊ COOK TIME: 13–15 MINS

WF | V | NF | SoF

2 **eggs**
150g **light brown sugar** (ideally muscovado)
225g good-quality **70% dark chocolate**
30g (2 tablespoons) **unsalted butter**
1 teaspoon **vanilla bean paste**
50g **wholegrain rye flour**
½ teaspoon **baking powder**
flaky sea salt, plus extra to decorate

Tartine is a bakery in San Francisco. Its original version of this recipe is rightly world famous. We've halved the quantities and dialled back the sugar. Wholegrain rye has a particularly high-fibre content, contains prebiotics and may help regulate blood sugar, and good-quality dark chocolate (at least 70%) is a great source of polyphenols, which also sustain our gut bacteria.

Whip the eggs in a stand mixer or using an electric whisk until really moussy, about 3 minutes. Gradually add the sugar, whisking to a thick golden mousse.

Set a heatproof bowl over a pan of just-simmering water. Add the chocolate, butter and vanilla, and melt together, ensuring the mixture doesn't get too hot and split. Sift the flour and baking powder together.

Fold the melted chocolate and the flour mixture into the eggs and add a pinch of salt. Fold until just mixed, being sure to scrape the sides and bottom of the bowl, as the chocolate may sink. Place in the fridge for 20 minutes, to firm up.

Heat the oven to 180°C/350°F/gas mark 4. Line 2 baking sheets with baking paper.

Use 2 spoons to drop small dollops of the mixture onto the baking sheets, leaving 5cm between each as the biscuits will spread. Scatter each with a tiny pinch of salt.

Bake in the oven for 8–10 minutes until spread out and slightly risen. They will seem slightly undercooked when you take them out, but don't worry, as long as they have puffed up, the top has just about set and you can't see raw, shiny dough, they're ready. Cool completely on the sheets before moving them as they will be fragile.

These store for a couple of days in an airtight container (if you manage to keep them that long, let us know!). They also freeze well.

≡TIP≡

You could broaden the micronutrient and fibre content of these cookies by adding a handful of finely chopped walnuts, hazelnuts, almonds or pecans, a mixture of all four, or some dried fruit, just before chilling the dough.

YOGHURT PANNA COTTA

SERVES 4

PREP TIME: 5 MINS ✳ COOK TIME: 10 MINS PLUS AT LEAST 4 HOURS CHILLING

WF | GF | NF | SoF

3 **gelatine leaves** (or V alternative,
   such as vege-gel – follow the packet
   instructions)
100ml **double** or **single cream**
100ml **milk of your choice**
½ teaspoon **vanilla bean paste**
50g **caster sugar**
300g **full-fat Greek yoghurt**
flavourless oil (such as **vegetable** or
   sunflower oil), for greasing (optional)
fresh or **frozen berries** (whizzed into a
   sauce with a pinch of **sugar** – optional),
   to serve

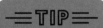

TIP

You can make this DF or Ve
by using a blend of dairy-free
yoghurt and coconut milk
(or experiment with other
plant-based milks) and vegan
gelatine alternatives, but
follow the packet instructions
carefully.

Panna cotta are like little wobbly milky jellies – great for kids and adults alike – and suit being made with live yoghurt. Using vanilla bean paste rather than extract means the mixture is prettily flecked with vanilla seeds.

Pour enough cold water over the gelatine leaves to cover. Set aside to soak.

Put the cream, milk, vanilla and sugar into a small pan and set over a low heat to warm through. Remove the pan from the heat. Remove the gelatine from the water and squeeze out any excess water, then add it to the cream mixture and stir until dissolved. Stir in the yoghurt.

If you want to turn out the puddings, grease the inside of your moulds very, very lightly with completely flavourless oil and add a circle of greaseproof paper to the bottom of each.

Divide the mixture between 4 moulds, ramekins or wine or cocktail glasses. Place in the fridge to set – this may happen in as little as a couple of hours, but allow about 4 hours, or overnight.

To turn out the puddings, fill a bowl with very hot water. Dip each mould into the water for a couple of seconds, making sure no water gets into the mould itself, then place a serving plate over the top of the mould. Quickly invert the mould and plate, and the pudding should gently plop onto the plate. If not, repeat, leaving in the hot water slightly longer. Take care – if you leave it too long, the exterior of the pudding will melt and lose its shape.

Serve with fresh berries, or a berry sauce made with frozen fruit and a pinch of sugar.

MANGO FROZEN YOGHURT

SERVES 4

PREP TIME: 5 MINS ✳ RESTING TIME: 3 HOURS

WF | GF | V | NF | SoF

250ml **full-fat Greek yoghurt**

1 small ripe **mango**, peeled and cut into small chunks

4 tablespoons **honey**

1 tablespoon **vanilla extract**

Frozen yoghurt without the expensive ice cream maker. Mango has lots of prebiotic fibres but practically any fruit will work for this – just make sure it is fully blended into the yoghurt mixture before transferring it to the dish. Taste for sweetness, as you will need more or less honey depending on the fruit. Double this recipe to make more for the freezer.

Combine all the ingredients in a food processor and blitz until completely smooth, pausing to scrape down the sides with a spatula from time to time. It should be light and fluffy and a lovely pale yellow colour. Taste and add more honey if you want it a little sweeter.

Using a spatula, transfer the mixture to a small glass baking dish. Cover with clingfilm and freeze for 1 hour.

Remove from the freezer, carefully peel back the clingfilm and stir the frozen edges into the soft middle, gently mixing it all together. This is to stop large ice crystals forming in the yoghurt. Spread the mixture out evenly, replace the clingfilm, and return to the freezer.

Repeat this process every 30 minutes for roughly 2 hours, or until it is the consistency you want to serve it at: either soft-serve yoghurt or firmer so you can scoop it into balls like ice cream.

=**TIP**=

Funnily enough, this freezes well. Just make sure you take it out 30 minutes before you want to eat it, as it needs that time to become soft enough to serve without needing a hammer.

SUPER SMOOTHIES

A good smoothie is all about balance – enough liquid so that it isn't too thick or too thin, enough fruit so that it has just the right level of sweetness, enough extras that you feel good after drinking it. If you think of these recipes as a guide, you can take your smoothie in all sorts of directions.

Each recipe here makes 1 large smoothie but can easily be doubled. For each recipe, just pop all the ingredients into a blender and whizz until completely smooth.

Optional extras you might like to experiment with include: ground cinnamon, turmeric, ginger or even cayenne pepper (chilli and chocolate have been paired for centuries); cocoa or cacoa powder (mix to a paste first to avoid lumps); matcha; ground seeds such as hemp or flax; tahini; ground maca root; oats or oat flour; ground coconut; nut butters or nuts such as walnuts or almonds; avocado...

GREEN SMOOTHIE

MAKES 1

PREP TIME: 2 MINS

WF | GF | DF | V | Ve | NF | SoF

150ml **unsweetened almond milk**

1 ripe **banana**

1 tablespoon **ground flaxseeds/linseeds**

1 tablespoon **almond butter**

1 large handful **baby spinach leaves**

1 large handful **frozen blueberries**

CHIA BLUEBERRY SMOOTHIE

MAKES 1

PREP TIME: 2 MINS

WF | GF | DF | V | Ve | SoF

150ml **unsweetened almond milk**

1 ripe **banana**

1 tablespoon **chia seeds**

100g **frozen blueberries**

SUNSHINE SMOOTHIE

MAKES 1
PREP TIME: 2 MINS
WF | GF | DF | V | Ve | NF | SoF

150ml **orange juice**
a handful each of **strawberries**,
   pineapple chunks and
   mango chunks

1 **passion fruit**, inside scooped
   out

BREAKFAST SMOOTHIE

MAKES 1
PREP TIME: 4 MINS
WF | GF | V | NF | SoF

150ml **milk** of your choice
1 ripe **banana**
100g **frozen fruit** (whatever you
   have – we like berries)

1 tablespoon **porridge oats**
1 teaspoon **honey**

MELISSA'S TWISTED WIT BEER

MAKES ABOUT 34 PINTS

PREP TIME: 1 HOUR, PLUS 2 WEEKS FERMENTING & 3 WEEKS RESTING * COOK TIME: 2 HOURS

DF | NF | SoF

15.06kg **sterilized water** (known as **'liquor'**, experienced brewers might like to add some minerals to change your water chemistry, see Tip), plus 19kg **sterilized water** to sparge

2.3 kg **crushed Pilsner malt**

2.0 kg **crushed flaked wheat**

0.5 kg **crushed flaked oats**

220g **rice hulls**

15g **whole coriander seeds**

3g **Sichuan peppercorns**

100g **mixed lemon, lime and orange zest**, peeled into strips with minimum pith

30g **East Kent Golding hop pellets** (approximately 4–5% alpha acids)

20g **Mandarina Bavaria hop pellets**

10g **Belgian wheat beer yeast** (well-hydrated)

Traditionally brewed beer can be as lively with microbes as yoghurt or kefir. So we asked our friend and beer writer Melissa Coles, to create a home-brew recipe:

'Making beer is both very simple, and incredibly hard. Sure, you can easily make a perfectly drinkable substance, but the alchemy of it is to pay attention to the details and trust your senses. This Belgian Wheat (or wit) is a very forgiving style, chosen because every time I look at that big vibrant orange in the LEON branding, I think of this beer … but that probably says more about me than it does anything else. I like to tinker round the edges of classics though, so I've added a few of my own ideas about spicing, using ingredients you might already have kicking around the kitchen, but don't hesitate to experiment. Want to add some chamomile tea? Why not? Maybe some cardamom? The only limit is your imagination. Just start with a light touch until you get a handle on how different flavours come through, and in what concentrations you like to taste them.'

This is a very easy beginner's recipe and there are lots of useful books, or videos online, for the uninitiated. You will need a 19-litre homebrew kit (comprising a beer kettle/big pan, a mash tun, a sparge set-up, a fermentation vessel and a thermometer) and a beer kettle, both readily available online with all the beer ingredients. You will also need a heat exchanger, a bubbler airlock for the top of your fermentation bucket, some food-safe sterilizer, a hydrometer and a large muslin bag with long strings (or a clean pair of tights!) For those who have made beer before, we are aiming for Original Gravity (OG) of around 1.053, Final Gravity (FG) of around 1.012, International Bittering Unit (IBU) of 20, a Standard Reference Measurement (SRM) colour level of 3 and Alcohol by Volume (ABV) of about 5%.

Heat the liquor to 72°C. Meanwhile, mix the grains together, making sure the rice hulls are evenly distributed throughout. This mix of grains is called the grist.

Add a small amount of water to the bottom of the mash tun and then start slowly adding your grains and heated liquor, stirring gently as you go, until it reaches a porridge-like consistency. When you have completed this 'mashing in' process, the temperature of the mash should be 65–67°C. Maintain for 90 minutes by wrapping the mash tun in old towels, or placing on an induction hob if you have one.

Whilst your mash is resting, start heating your sparging liquor. After 90 minutes, raise the temperature of your mash to about 75°C if possible (not wholly necessary but a good step to take). Re-circulate slightly by running off some wort (the sweet liquid that has resulted from the conversion of starch into sugar during mashing in) from the bottom of the mash tun and pouring it back into the top, until the wort is running fairly clear out of the bottom of the mash tun.

Now it is time to 'sparge' (push some of the sugars out of the mash). The water dilutes the sugars to the appropriate amount for the ABV you're aiming for. Place the beer kettle (or big pan) below the mash tun and open the valve of the mash tun to begin draining the wort into the beer kettle. Add the sparge liquid to the top of the mash tun to run through the mash, collecting it all. When you are sparging, wait until you have a good couple of inches in the bottom of the kettle (or, if you have a fancier set up, when it covers the elements) before you switch the heat on to boil it.

Boil the collected wort for 90 minutes in a well-ventilated space, a cooker hood on full blast will do. This concentrates the beer's flavours, makes it sterile and prevents unwanted dimethyl sulphide (which gives a horrible over-boiled veg note to beer).

While the wort is boiling, heat the oven to 120°C. Crush the coriander seeds and peppercorns lightly, in a pestle and mortar, and place them on an oven tray with the

LOWER SUGAR (BUT STILL SWEET)

citrus peels. Place in the oven and toast for 8–10 minutes or until you can just smell the aromas. Remove from the oven and tip everything into the clean muslin bag.

After 60 minutes, add the East Kent Golding hop pellets to the beer kettle and leave for another 25 minutes. Then add the Madarina Bavaria hop pellets to the beer kettle and suspend your muslin spice bag in the liquid, ensuring it doesn't sit on the bottom or near any elements. Leave it in for the final 5 minutes.

Once the 5 minutes is up (so the wort has been boiling for 90 minutes in total), use the heat ex-changer to chill the wort as quickly as possible. Leave the spice bag in for the first 10 minutes, removing it only when it's cool enough to safely handle. Allow the cold break material (protein-based gunk which has broken out of the solution) to settle at the bottom of the kettle, then slowly pour the liquid into your sterilized fermentation bucket. Don't worry too much about disturbing the layer of cold break at the bottom, as it will add some signature cloudiness to the beer.

Use a sterilized whisk to aerate the wort in the fermenter and, as the liquid is still moving, add (or 'pitch') the yeast into the wort. Seal the bucket and pop the airlock in the top so you can see if it's fermenting happily or not, then leave somewhere with a temperature of approximately 18°C for one week, After the week is up, slowly raise the temperature of the room (or cupboard) over the next week to 23°C.

After two weeks fermenting, you can package the beer in a home brew-sized sterile keg. Follow the packet instructions to achieve a 'soft carbonation level' of 2–2.5 volumes of CO_2. Alternatively, you can bottle condition it by pitching a small amount of yeast and a tiny amount of sugar in every bottle. (The exact amount of both will vary according to your to bottle size).

Finally, let it rest for a week at a room temperature of around 16°C and then for a couple of weeks somewhere very cold. Then open and enjoy with pals!

HOMEBREWED GINGER BEER

MAKES 1 LITRE

PREP TIME: 5 MINS PLUS UP TO 7 DAYS FERMENTING

WF | GF | DF | V | Ve | NF | SoF

1 litre **water**

¼ teaspoon **cream of tartar**

juice of 1 **lemon** or **orange**

125g **sugar**

2 tablespoons chopped **fresh ginger** (we peel the ginger then slice into short matchsticks so it's easy to separate from the ginger 'plant' afterwards), or more as needed

about 1 tablespoon **active ginger beer plant**

a pinch of **ground ginger** (optional)

For real ginger beer – which, beware, can be up to 5% ABV – you need a ginger 'plant' – a special combination of yeast and bacteria for making ginger beer. You can buy one online and store in the fridge for 1–2 weeks between uses. You must activate it first, if it has been stored for a while. It may come with specific instructions, but you usually need to give it a couple of tablespoons of sugar, in about 250ml water, with ½ teaspoon of cream of tartar or a squeeze of lemon juice. Leave for 24 hours, strain the plant out, discard the liquid, then start the recipe below.

In a glass jug or large jar, stir everything except the ginger beer plant and ground ginger together. Once the sugar and cream of tartar are fully dissolved, stir in the ginger beer plant. Cover the jug/jar with kitchen paper, a clean tea towel or a piece of muslin and secure with a rubber band or string. Don't seal it. Leave somewhere with a steady temperature, out of direct sunlight, for about 48 hours. (Don't store close to anything else you're fermenting as cross contamination of bacteria can occur.)

Strain the liquid into a jug, keeping the solids. With clean hands, remove and discard the ginger, but keep the ginger plant. Taste. Is it gingery enough? You can add a little grated fresh ginger or some ground ginger, if you think it needs more oomph.

Pour into a clean 1-litre fizzy drinks bottle and seal with a lid. Ginger beer can get really fizzy, so don't store it in anything that might explode. Leave the bottle, again out of sunlight, for 3–4 days, or until the bottle feels firm to the touch.

Chill in the fridge before drinking. Be careful when you open the bottle as it may fizz uncontrollably!

≡TIP≡

If you prefer, use ground ginger instead of root – this will give a spicier, sharper end result.

LOWER SUGAR (BUT STILL SWEET)

SWITCHEL

SERVES 2
PREP TIME: 2 MINS
WF | GF | DF | V | Ve | NF | SoF

4cm piece of **fresh ginger**, peeled

2 teaspoons **raw, unpasteurized apple cider vinegar** (with mother), plus extra to taste

2 teaspoons **maple syrup**, **agave** or **honey** (use **maple syrup** or **agave** if Ve), plus extra to taste

1 tablespoon **freshly squeezed lemon juice**

TO SERVE:
ice
still or **sparkling water**

Switchel, a tangy, gingery drink, has been around for a couple of hundred years, but recently became trendy – in part because it contains live microbes. Rebecca drank switchels when she was pregnant and searching for something that was more interesting than water but not sugary and sweet. If you don't like ginger's spiciness, leave it out. We hear tell that this is good as a mixer, with whisky or vodka, but we couldn't possibly comment...

Grate the ginger into a small bowl, then transfer to a fine sieve (or a regular sieve lined with some muslin). Use the back of a spoon to press the juices through into a jug. Add the maple syrup, agave or honey, the apple cider vinegar and lemon juice. Stir together.

Divide between 2 glasses filled with ice. Top up with still or sparkling water, but leave space at the top of the glass. Taste – you may want more vinegar or more sweetness. Switchel should be tart and zingy, but not mouth-puckeringly sharp. Keep adjusting until it's just right – being precise is tricky as some vinegars have a lot of natural sweetness while others are extremely sour. The end result shouldn't feel harsh in your mouth or throat. Keep a note of what you do, so you can make it again.

=TIP=
Garnish with mint and serve as a non-alcoholic cocktail.

CONVERSION CHARTS

LINEAR CONVERSIONS

2mm	1/16 inch	6cm	2½ inches	18cm	7 inches	33cm	13 inches
3mm	⅛ inch	7cm	2¾ inches	19cm	7½ inches	34cm	13½ inches
5mm	¼ inch	8cm	3¼ inches	20cm	8 inches	35cm	14 inches
8mm	⅜ inch	9cm	3½ inches	22cm	8½ inches	37cm	14½ inches
10mm/1cm	½ inch	9.5cm	3¾ inches	23cm	9 inches	38cm	15 inches
15mm	⅝ inch	10cm	4 inches	24cm	9½ inches	39cm	15½ inches
2cm	¾ inch	11cm	4¼ inches	25cm	10 inches	40cm	16 inches
2.5cm	1 inch	12cm	4½ inches	26cm	10½ inches	42cm	16½ inches
3cm	1¼ inches	13cm	5 inches	27cm	10¾ inches	43cm	17 inches
4cm	1½ inches	14cm	5½ inches	28cm	11 inches	44cm	17½ inches
4.5cm	1¾ inches	15cm	6 inches	29cm	11½ inches	46cm	18 inches
5cm	2 inches	16cm	6¼ inches	30cm	12 inches	48cm	19 inches
5.5cm	2¼ inches	17cm	6½ inches	31cm	12½ inches	50cm	20 inches

VOLUME CONVERSIONS

Use teaspoon measures for measures under 5ml when possible.

1.25ml	¼ tsp	450ml	15¼ fl oz
2.5ml	½ tsp	473ml	1 pint
5ml	1 tsp	500ml	17fl oz
10ml	2 tsp	550ml	18½fl oz
15ml	1 tbsp / 3 tsp / ½fl oz	591ml	1¼ pints
30ml	2 tbsp / 1fl oz	600ml	20¼fl oz
45ml	3 tbsp	650ml	22fl oz
50ml	1¾fl oz	700ml	23¾fl oz
60ml	4 tbsp	710ml	1½ pints
75ml	5 tbsp / 2½fl oz	750ml	25¼fl oz
90ml	6 tbsp	828ml	1¾ pints
100ml	3½fl oz	850ml	28¾fl oz
125ml	4¼fl oz	946ml	2 pints
150ml	5fl oz	1 litre	33¾fl oz
175ml	6fl oz	1.2 litres	2½ pints
200ml	6¾fl oz	1.3 litres	2¾ pints
225ml	7½fl oz	1.4 litres	3 pints
250ml	8½fl oz	1.7 litres	3½ pints
300ml	10¼fl oz	2 litres	4¼ pints
350ml	11¾fl oz	2.5 litres	5¼ pints
400ml	13½fl oz	2.8 litres	6 pints
425ml	14¼fl oz	3 litres	6¼ pints

WEIGHT CONVERSIONS

5g	⅛oz	375g	13oz
10g	¼oz	400g	14oz
15g	½oz	425g	15oz
25/30g	1oz	450g	1lb
35g	1¼oz	500g	1lb 2oz
40g	1½oz	550g	1lb 4oz
50g	1¾oz	600g	1lb 5oz
55g	2oz	650g	1lb 7oz
60g	2¼oz	700g	1lb 9oz
70g	2½oz	750g	1lb 10oz
85g	3oz	800g	1lb 12oz
90g	3¼oz	850g	1lb 14oz
100g	3½oz	900g	2lb
115g	4oz	950g	2lb 1½oz
125g	4½oz	1kg	2lb 4oz
140g	5oz	1.25kg	2lb 12oz
150g	5½oz	1.3kg	3lb
175g	6oz	1.5kg	3lb 5oz
200g	7oz	1.6kg	3lb 8oz
225g	8oz	1.8kg	4lb
250g	9oz	2kg	4lb 8oz
275g	9¼oz	2.25kg	5lb
280g	10oz	2.5kg	5lb 8oz
300g	10½oz	2.7kg	6lb
325g	11½oz	3kg	6lb 8oz
350g	12oz		

GLOSSARY

UK	US	UK	US
apple purée	applesauce	grill, grill pan	broiler, broiler pan
aubergine	eggplant	ground almonds	almond meal
baking paper	parchment paper	hob	stove top
beetroot	beet	jug	liquid measuring cup or pitcher
bicarbonate of soda	baking soda	kitchen paper	paper towels
blitz/whizz	to process in a food processor or blender	loaf tin	loaf pan; a 900g/2lb pan is about 9 x 5 x 3 inches
brine	a salt-based liquid	mange tout	snow peas
broad beans	fava beans	muslin	cheesecloth
caster sugar	superfine sugar	pak choi	bok choy
celeriac	celery root	pepper (e.g., red pepper)	bell pepper
charcuterie	deli meats	plain flour	all-purpose flour
chestnut mushroom	cremini mushroom	polenta	cornmeal
chicory	Belgian endive	porridge oats	rolled oats
chilli flakes	dried red pepper flakes	prawns	shrimp
chopping board	cutting board	rapeseed oil	canola oil
clingfilm	plastic wrap	rocket	arugula
cooker hood	kitchen extractor fan	shallow-fry	pan-fry
coriander, fresh	cilantro	sieve	strainer
courgette	zucchini	single cream	light cream
dark chocolate	semisweet chocolate (or bittersweet if more than 70% cocoa)	skewer	use a toothpick
		spring onion	scallion; green onion
dessertspoon	soup spoon or tablespoon	steak, rump/sirloin	steak, sirloin/tenderloin
double cream	heavy cream	stick blender	immersion blender
easy-bake yeast	active dry yeast	strong flour	bread flour
egg, medium	U.S. large egg	sultanas	golden raisins
fish finger	fish stick	sweetcorn	corn kernels
fish sauce	Thai fish sauce	tea towel	dish towel
fizzy drink	soft drink	tenderstem broccoli	broccolini
flaked almonds	slivered almonds	tick list	check list
full-fat (yoghurt/milk)	whole	tomato purée	tomato paste
gelatine leaves	gelatin sheets	whisk, electric	mixer, electric handheld
glass/thread noodles	cellophane noodles	white cabbage	use green cabbage
gram flour	chickpea (besan) flour	wholemeal flour	whole-wheat flour

INDEX

ABOUT THE AUTHORS

REBECCA SEAL

Rebecca has written about food and drink for the *Financial Times*, *Evening Standard*, the *Observer*, the *Guardian*, *Red* and *The Sunday Times*. Her most recent – and first non-food book – is called *SOLO: How To Work Alone (And Not Lose Your Mind)*. Her cookbooks include *Istanbul: Recipes from the heart of Turkey* and *Lisbon: Recipes from the heart of Portugal*, as well as co-authoring *LEON Happy Soups*, *LEON Happy One-pot Cooking*, *LEON Fast Vegan*, *LEON Happy Curries* and *LEON Happy Fast Food* with John Vincent. She is one of the food and drink experts on Channel 4's *Sunday Brunch*. She lives in London with her husband and two small daughters.

JOHN VINCENT

John is co-founder of LEON, which now has 74 restaurants (including in Amsterdam, Utrecht, Oslo and Washington, DC). He wrote *LEON Naturally Fast Food* with Henry Dimbleby, *LEON Family & Friends* with Kay Plunkett-Hogge, *LEON Happy Salads* and *LEON Fast & Free* with Jane Baxter and *LEON Happy Soups*, *LEON Happy One-pot Cooking*, *LEON Fast Vegan*, *LEON Happy Curries* and *LEON Happy Fast Food* with Rebecca Seal. He thinks that our relationship with food should be positive and joyous and that we need to listen more carefully to our gut, eat more good fats and less sugar.

ACKNOWLEDGEMENTS

FROM REBECCA:

The Happy LEON cookbooks are always a team effort (as well as being a huge joy to work on) and it was particularly special to bring a team together in 2020, a time when work was harder to do, and restaurants were having to reinvent themselves over and again in order to keep going. We were all very grateful that we were able to carry on working, safely, together and felt very lucky to be a small part of LEON, at a time when the business was working incredibly hard to feed people working in the NHS and on the frontline, as well as pivoting in order to keep its customers well fed. I know I speak for the whole book team when I say we were very proud to be associated with a business that worked so tirelessly to do so much good in 2020. Thanks for having us with you, John.

I would like to thank Steven Joyce (and not only because he's my husband!) for his beautiful photography and his brilliant assistants Amy Grinstead, Tom Groves and Matthew Hague. Thanks to Lauren Law for art direction and props styling. Rosie Reynolds was our food stylist extraordinaire and, along with her wonderful assistant Toni Musgrave, made everything look delectable and helped finesse some of the recipes, too. (Special thanks also to Kitty Coles who cooked for some very early pages of the book.) Thanks to Jack Burke, who helped me with some last-minute recipe testing when I was flailing under the weight of deadlines and lack of childcare. Kelly Rigg helped sort through all the nutritional info for each recipe. As ever, the Octopus team makes it all feel much easier than it really is: thanks to Alison Starling and Pauline Bache for making sure the book came together, to Emily Preece-Morrison for sharpening up the text, to Ella Mclean and Sean Matthews for the design, and to Samantha Gill for helping us avoid any nutritional howlers.

FROM JOHN:

Rebecca has thanked many of the people in our wider team, and I would like to echo her words. I would also like to single out Rebecca herself for particular gratitude and praise. Rebecca is an intelligent, sparky, creative and collaborative partner. I would recommend her to others, but tbh, would rather keep her to myself. I think this is a lovely and important book that will make people happier and healthier. This is made possible by the magic and method of Rebecca Seal and her teammate and husband Steve. So, thank you Rebecca. And thank you teammate Steve. Again soon, please.

An Hachette UK Company
www.hachette.co.uk

First published in Great Britain in 2021 by Conran Octopus,
an imprint of
Octopus Publishing Group Ltd
Carmelite House
50 Victoria Embankment
London EC4Y 0DZ
www.octopusbooks.co.uk

Distributed in the US by Hachette Book Group
1290 Avenue of the Americas
4th and 5th Floors, New York, NY 10104

Distributed in Canada by Canadian Manda Group
664 Annette Street, Toronto, Ontario, Canada M6S 2C8

ISBN 978-1-84091-802-1

A CIP catalogue record for this book is available from the British Library.

Printed and bound in China

10 9 8 7 6 5 4 3 2 1

Photography by Steven Joyce

Publisher: Alison Starling
Creative director: Jonathan Christie
Senior editor: Pauline Bache
Senior production controller: Emily Noto

Food stylist: Rosie Reynolds
Food styling assistant: Toni Musgrave
Prop stylist: Lauren Law
Photography assistants: Amy Grinstead, Tom Groves, Matthew Hague
Designer: Ella Mclean
LEON lead designer: Sean Matthews
LEON head of marketing: Rebecca Di Mambro
Photography on endpapers courtesy of LEON, Tom Groves and Lauren Law

We have endeavoured to be as accurate as possible in all the preparation
and cooking times listed in the recipes in this book. However, they are an
estimate based on our own timings during recipe testing, and should be
taken as a guide only, not as the literal truth.

Nutrition advice is not absolute. If you feel you require consultation with
a nutritionist, consult your GP for a recommendation.

Standard level spoon measurements are used in all recipes.
1 tablespoon = one 15ml spoon
1 teaspoon = one 5ml spoon

Eggs should be medium unless otherwise stated and preferably free
range and organic. The Department of Health advises that eggs should
not be consumed raw. This book contains dishes made with raw or lightly
cooked eggs. It is prudent for more vulnerable people such as pregnant
and nursing mothers, invalids, the elderly, babies and young children to
avoid uncooked or lightly cooked dishes made with eggs. Once prepared
these dishes should be kept refrigerated and used promptly.

Fresh herbs should be used unless otherwise stated. If unavailable, use
dried herbs as an alternative but halve the quantities stated.

Ovens should be preheated to the specific temperature – if using a fan-
assisted oven, follow manufacturer's instructions for adjusting the time
and the temperature.

This book includes dishes made with nuts and nut derivatives. It is
advisable for customers with known allergic reactions to nuts and nut
derivatives and those who may be potentially vulnerable to these allergies,
such as babies and children with a family history of allergies, to avoid
dishes made with nuts and nut oils. It is also prudent to check the labels of
pre-prepared ingredients for the possible inclusion of nut derivatives.

Vegetarians should look for the 'V' symbol on a cheese to ensure it is
made with vegetarian rennet.

Not all soy sauce is gluten-free – we use tamari (a gluten-free type of soy
sauce), but check the label if you are unsure.

Remember to check the labels on ingredients to make sure they don't
have hidden refined sugars. Even savoury goods can be artificially
sweetened so it's always best to check the label carefully.